HUMOROUS NOTES,
QUOTES, AND ANECDOTES

HUMOROUS NOTES, QUOTES, AND ANECDOTES

Leslie & Bernice Flynn

BAKER BOOK HOUSE
Grand Rapids, Michigan

AGE

☐ "There are two signs of old age," said the professor. "One is forgetfulness." He paused. "The second sign is. . . . I guess I've forgotten it."

☐ Every five years a photographer was hired to do an expensive portrait of a wealthy matron. All went well for several years. But on her sixtieth birthday, she indignantly returned the proofs, claiming, "This picture is not nearly as good as the one you took five years ago."

Looking at the proofs for a few moments, the photographer sighed sadly, "Well, I'm not the man I was five years ago!"

☐ Little boy: Grandpa, were you on the ark?
Grandpa: Of course not!
Little boy: Then how come you weren't drowned?

☐ Photographer (after taking picture of a man on his ninety-sixth birthday): I hope I'm still around to take your picture on your one hundredth birthday.

Old man: I don't see why you won't. You look pretty healthy.

☐ A reporter asked a man on his ninety-fifth birthday, "To what do you credit your long life?"

"Not sure yet," responded the old-timer. "My lawyer's negotiating with two breakfast cereal companies."

☐ A magazine feature writer, interviewing a lady on her one-hundredth birthday, asked, "How did you live so long?"

"Well," she whined, "I never did the dishes in our house. I never washed the floors nor did the housecleaning. I never got up at night with our ten children. My dear Henry did that. May he rest in peace; he died when he was forty-six."

☐ A lady had just returned from an overseas trip with her husband, an archaeologist. A friend asked the wife, "How do you like being married to a man who studies antiquities?"

Came the answer, "Think of it this way. An archaeologist makes a good husband. The older I get, the more he's interested in me."

☐ Little boy: Did you hear about the eighty-eight-year-old man and the seventy-nine-year-old lady that got married last week?

Little girl: Did they throw rice at them?

Little boy: No, they threw vitamins.

☐ Lady to doctor: I've no trouble hearing; but I do have a little difficulty these days overhearing.

☐ A couple celebrated their wedding anniversary every year by taking the train to the country inn where they had spent their honeymoon, always returning home the same evening.

On their fiftieth trip they just missed the last train home by a few seconds. Forced to stay at the inn for the night, they were about to retire. Combing her silver hair, the elderly wife said to her husband, "There's summer in my heart, and winter in my hair."

Replied the husband, "If you had spring in your feet we would never have missed that train."

☐ At a college reunion thirty years after graduation one man said to another, "See that fellow over there. Well—he's gotten so bald and so fat he didn't even recognize me."

☐ A little boy visited the big city for the first time. Intrigued by the elevators, he stood in front of one for several minutes. He saw an old lady, slow-moving and wrinkled, enter. The light flashed, the door closed, and she was gone. A minute later to his amazement the same door opened and out stepped a pretty, peppy young lady. As he turned to leave, he could be heard mumbling, "I'm going to tell grandpa to bring grandma here."

☐ Officer: The minute I saw you from my parked patrol car I figured you were approaching sixty.
Lady: How dare you talk that way! I'm still in my thirties.

ALMOST

☐ A chemist concocted a soft-drink formula and called it *one-up*. But it didn't sell. He tried to improve it, and changed the name to *two-up*. Still it didn't sell. Again he revised the formula and the name to *three-up*. Still, it was a failure. He kept trying till he called his product *six-up*. Still no success. Then he quit.

ANCESTORS

☐ An aristocratic Southern lady was invited to a Sunday school class where the subject was Bible history. That morning the teacher centered attention on the ancient Medes and Persians. After fifty minutes of what he thought was clear, acceptable instruction, his bubble was burst when the Southern lady, greeting him with hand outstretched at the door, drawled, "I did so enjoy your lesson. You know —my grandmother was a Mead!"

☐ A little boy was bragging up his family pedigree. "Why, my ancestors came over on the *Mayflower!* They were among the first to come across!"
Another little boy whose father ran the corner grocery store retorted, "My dad says your folks are among the last to come across!"

☐ A social climber in the aristocratic Episcopalian church paid a researcher one hundred dollars to dig into his family tree. Not only does he no longer have interest in his ancestral pedigree, but he had to pay the researcher another hundred dollars to keep him silent.

☐ A lawyer discovered that one of his ancestors had been hanged for cattle stealing. To hide the fact, he rewrote his family history thus, "Grandfather died while taking part in a public ceremony—when the platform gave way."

☐ Discovering that one of her progenitors had died in the electric chair, a New England aristocratic told her fine friends, "Great Uncle Ezekiel occupied the chair of applied electricity in one of the great institutions of this country. He died in harness."

☐ At a party, one lady, boasting of her ancestry, cooed, "It goes back to the days of William the Conqueror." Then turning to a woman sitting nearby she asked with an air of superiority, "How far does your family go back?"

"I really don't know," the woman responded, "because all of our records were lost in the Flood."

☐ First friend: Some families can trace their ancestors back two hundred years.

Second friend: And others can't tell you where their children were last night.

☐ An aspiring socialite sat between a rabbi and a minister at a fund-raising dinner. Proud of her position between the clerics, she gushed, "I feel as though I were a leaf between the Old and New Testaments with my genealogy written thereon."

"That page," replied the clergyman, "is usually blank."

☐ A man was asked if his ancestors came over on the *Mayflower*. "No," he sighed, "but they were there to meet the ship."

ANIMALS

☐ Dog 1: I don't feel very well. I'm tired all the time.
Dog 2: Have you ever thought of seeing a psychiatrist?
Dog 1: Of course not. You know I'm not allowed on couches.

☐ The phone rang in the office of a theatrical booking agent. "Hello," said a voice. "I want a job. I can sing, dance, and juggle."

"So can a thousand other people—and they're all out of work," snapped the agent.

"Just a minute—don't hang up. I can play the piano, walk a tightrope, and recite Lincoln's Gettysburg Address backward."

"So can all those others. You're wasting my time."

"Just a minute," pleaded the voice. "There's one other thing. I'm a dog!"

☐ A little girl visiting a farm on a Sunday school outing saw her first sow. It was a huge animal squatting in the pigpen. The farmer commented, "Big, isn't she?"

"She ought to be," exclaimed the little girl. "I saw her a few minutes ago and she had eight little ones blowing her up."

☐ A little girl, petting a kitten: "She must be talking to somebody—I can hear the busy signal."

☐ During a TV program a dog, a Great Dane, would nod knowingly to its master at humorous incidents. A visitor, amazed, exclaimed to the master, "Why, your dog seems to enjoy the program and even like its humor!"

"I'm surprised too," the master replied, "because he didn't like it a bit when it appeared in book form."

9

☐ A visitor at a zoo was surprised to see a lion and a lamb in the same cage. He asked the attendant if they got along all right.

He replied, "Most of the time, but now and again we have to put in a new lamb."

☐ A little boy when asked to explain the meanings of "wholesale" and "retail" thought up this: "If a horse had his tail cut off, in order to 'wholesale' him, you would first have to 're-tail' him."

☐ Mama Skunk worried because she couldn't keep track of her two children whose names were In and Out. One day she called Out in to her and told him to go out and bring In back. So Out went out and soon brought In in. "How could you find him so quickly in this great forest?"

"It was simple," said Out. "In stinct."

☐ A man claimed he had a Christian horse. It had been trained to go forward, not on Giddap, but on "Praise the Lord," and to halt, not on "Whoa," but on "Amen." A friend who borrowed the horse was informed of these key words. Suddenly, as they neared a steep precipice, the man in his excitement roared, "Whoa!" But the horse kept right on trotting. Just in the nick of time the man remembered and shouted, "Amen."

The horse stopped on the brink of the cliff. With a sigh of relief, the rider exclaimed, "Praise the Lord."

☐ A missionary traveling through the jungle met a lion. Escape was impossible; so the missionary fell to his knees in prayer. A few minutes later he was greatly comforted to see the lion on his knees beside him.

"Dear brother," said the relieved missionary, "how delightful to join you in prayer, when a moment ago I despaired of my life."

"Don't interrupt," said the lion. "I'm saying grace!"

ANNOUNCEMENTS

☐ A lady whose husband had just reenlisted in the navy sent her preacher a hurried note during the church service, with a request for prayer. The note said, "John Smith, having gone to sea, his wife desires the prayers of the congregation for his safety."

The minister read the note hastily. Here is how he announced it. "John Smith having gone to see his wife, desires the prayers of the congregation for his safety."

☐ A little girl went to church for the first time. After the service the minister asked how she had liked it. "Well," she thought for a moment, "I thought the music was very fine; but your commercial was too long!"

☐ When making the announcements, a minister had the peculiar habit of placing his thumbs in his vest pockets and patting his stomach with his hands. One Sunday he said, "Monday night will be teachers' meeting." Then he patted his stomach. "Wednesday will be midweek service." Again he patted his stomach. "And Friday we're going to have a great dinner." And he patted his stomach. Then while continuing the patting he added, "The purpose of this feed is to enlarge this place."

☐ A couple arrived at the church study just five minutes before the morning service was to begin. "We'd like to get married," they explained. "I can't do it right now," said the pastor, "but when it comes announcement time in the middle of the service, I'll ask anyone who wants to get married to come forward. You come right up front and I'll marry you."

At announcement time the pastor intoned, "Anyone here want to get married? Please come up front."

Immediately three bachelors and twenty-three spinsters came forward.

ATHEISM

☐ An atheist said to a little boy, "I'll give you an orange if you can tell me one place where God is."

The boy replied, "I'll give you two oranges if you can tell me one place where God is not."

☐ A few years ago an American guard in Berlin next to the Russian sector neared the end of his daily stint of duty. Taking out his watch, he sighed, "Only a few minutes more, thank God."

At the same time a Russian guard looked at his watch and said, "Yes, time will soon be up, thank Brezhnev."

"What would you say," the American asked, "If Brezhnev were dead?"

The Russian replied, "Then I, too, would say, 'Thank God.' "

☐ A middle-aged playboy suddenly dropped dead one night on New York's East Side. He had been living it up. The doctor called to the scene examined the formally attired body, then questioned members of his party. He was told name, age, and address. Then the doctor asked the religion of the deceased.

"He was an atheist," someone answered.

The doctor looked down again at the white-tie-and-tails. "What a pity," he drawled. "All dressed up and no place to go."

☐ The new resident in the housing development didn't lose any time letting people know he was an atheist. Meeting a new neighbor for the first time he would introduce himself, mention he was a research chemist, then say, "There's no need to believe in the supernatural. For example, we can make rain now. We just send a fellow up in a plane. He drops some chemicals on a cloud, and presto—it rains."

One day a neighbor's eight-year-old girl piped up, "Who made the cloud?"

BAD COMPANY

☐ A farmer was troubled with crows. He finally decided to get his gun and scare them off. While they were eating in a field of grain he shot his gun into the midst of them. All flew away except one bird. When he went to get it he saw that it was his pet parrot that had escaped from its cage and had joined the crows. Picking it up he said, "Oh, Polly, this is the result of your keeping bad company." Carrying it in his coat he met his little girl.

"Did you shoot any crows?" she asked.

"I've shot Polly," he replied.

"Oh, daddy, how did you do that?"

Polly stuck her head out from under the coat and said, "Bad company, bad company!"

BIBLE

☐ A ladies' Bible class was having a weekday meeting in the home of one of their members. The gathering was held on the same day that the cleaning woman came. But that particular day she was ill. and sent a friend in her place. As the devotions were about to begin, the leader said to the hostess, "I came away without my Bible today. Could I borrow yours?"

The hostess hurried to get her Bible, but couldn't find it. She knew where it was, for she had used it the day before. But it wasn't anywhere to be found. She searched everywhere. The noise of opening and shutting drawers reached the women. "What will they think of me?" wondered the embarrassed hostess. In panic she ran down to the kitchen where the cleaning woman was at work. "Did you see anything of my Bible?" she asked breathlessly.

"Oh, praise the Lord!" exclaimed the cleaning lady.

"What do you mean?"

"Praise the Lord!" she continued. "The first thing I do when I start working for someone is to hide their Bible."

"But why?"

"Just to see how long it takes the people there to miss it. Yours is in the linen closet."

☐ A clergyman was delighted at the sudden spurt of interest shown in the Bible by a young housewife who came to church spasmodically. She had just phoned to ask for another word for the Ten Commandments. "Decalogue," said the pastor.

"It's so nice of you to tell me," she replied airily. "Now if that quiz program calls me today, I'm good for at least ten thousand dollars."

☐ A judge said to a woman pleading innocent to a minor charge, "If you can say the Lord's Prayer, you may go free."

She replied, "Now I lay me down to sleep; I pray the Lord my soul to keep."

He responded, "You may go free!"

☐ Teacher: What were the Phoenicians known for?
Pupil: Blinds.

☐ Until the end of the 1930's it was compulsory at Oxford University, England, for every student to pass a divinity course.

When a most promising athlete entered Oxford, the college had prospects of winning the league championship. His presence or absence on the Rugby team meant the difference between victory or defeat. But the star player just could not pass the divinity course. He had tried so often that at last it was decided that his final chance had come. But the governing board decided that if he could answer one question orally, all would be well for him and the Rugby team and the honor of Oxford.

So he was brought before a board of examiners. The question was put to him, "Who was the first king of Israel?" The moment was tense. As the silence grew longer all hopes of the Rugby team seemed to fade. Finally, the hesitant athlete blurted out, "Saul."

"Absolutely correct," answered the relieved professors. "That's all we need to ask. You may leave."

At the door, the uncertain athlete turned to his examiners. "But, sirs, I should have added, that it was Saul who afterwards was named Paul."

☐ A preacher one Saturday afternoon made the mistake of showing some boys the Bible lesson he was going to read in the service Sunday morning. When the preacher wasn't looking the boys glued the connecting pages together. Next morning he read on the bottom of one page, "And Noah, when he was one hundred and twenty years old, took himself a wife who was" . . . turning the page, "three hundred cubits long, fifty cubits wide, thirty cubits high, built of gopher wood, and pitched within and without with pitch."

Puzzled, he stopped. He read it a second time. Pausing again, he said, "Beloved, this is the first time I ever read this in the Bible; but I believe the Bible to be true from cover to cover. So I accept it as evidence that we are fearfully and wonderfully made."

☐ An American lady on a flying visit to the Holy Land came to a tourist office to ask for some information on motor roads in Israel. She was informed by one of the clerks that it was now possible to go by car all the way from Dan to Beersheba.

"Do you know," she replied, "I never knew that Dan and Beersheba were places. I always thought they were husband and wife like Sodom and Gomorrah!"

☐ A boy recently converted by reading the New Testament in his own dialect came to the missionary in much distress. "Sir, my big watchdog just got hold of the Testament and tore a page out of it."

The missionary tried to comfort him. "We can get another Testament. Don't worry!"

But the boy would not be consoled. "Think of the dog."

Supposing that the boy thought the paper would do the dog harm, the missionary laughed, "If your dog can crunch an ox-bone, he isn't going to be hurt by a piece of paper."

"Oh, sir," cried the boy, "I was once a bad boy. If I had an enemy, I hated him and everything in me wanted to kill him. Then I got the New Testament in my heart, and began to love everybody and forgive all my enemies. Now the dog, the great, big hunting dog, has got the Book in him, and will begin to love the lions and the tigers and let them help themselves to the sheep and oxen!"

☐ A magazine editor received a phone call from one of his authors. "How about a story on Pilate's wife?" he was asked. His reply: "Sorry, but we're overstocked with flying stories now."

☐ Wife: Who was this Joan of Arc that saved France?

Husband: You have those characters mixed up. It was Noah of Ark. Jonah's the man that swallowed the whale.

☐ The minister was visiting in one of his parishioner's homes. "So you attend Sunday school regularly?" he asked the little girl.

"Oh, yes, sir, every week," Susie replied.

"And do you know what's in the Bible?"

"Sure do. Sister's boyfriend's picture's in it. And Ma's recipe for chocolate cake's in it. And a lock of my hair cut off when I was a baby is in it. And besides, the pawn ticket for father's watch is in it."

☐ A preacher announced that he would speak on the story of the multitude that loafs and fishes.

☐ An American engineer working on a Pacific island met a native seated near a boiling pot, and to the American's surprise the native was reading a Bible.

"Back in America, we gave that Book up long ago. Few people really believe it now."

Replied the native, "It's a good thing the Bible reached here before you did; for if it hadn't, you would be in that big pot right now—roasting!"

BIRTHDAY

☐ First boy: Do your parents celebrate their birthdays?

Second boy: They certainly do. Father takes a day off and mother takes a year off.

☐ First husband: Is your wife economical?
   Second husband: On her birthdays. She used only forty candles on her fiftieth birthday cake.

☐ Math teacher: How old would a person be who was born in 1910?
   Pupil: Man or woman?

☐ A young man fell for a lovely young lady, and anticipated soon popping the question. On her birthday he ordered a rose for every year of her life. The florist took his order for twenty-two roses, then thought to himself, "He's one of my steadiest customers. I'll make him more popular with his girl and send thirty-two." The young man never found out why she turned down his proposal.

BOASTING

☐ An ant crossed a bridge on the back of an elephant. After a safe but noisy crossing, the ant exclaimed, "My, didn't we shake that bridge!"

☐ 1st boy: What is boasting?
   2nd boy: Blowing off a little self-esteem.
   3rd boy: Pushing yourself forward by patting yourself on the back.

☐ Back when organs were pumped by hand, a famous organist, leaving the platform after a program, said to himself, "I really did some excellent work this evening. I don't know when I ever played better." The boy who had pumped the wind frowned at the artist.

   The next evening, the artist placed his hands on the keys, but there was no sound. He tried again. No response. Scowling fiercely at the pumper, the artist indicated wind was needed.

   The boy grinned and admonished, "Say 'we,' mister."

☐ One afternoon the German author Goethe and the composer Beethoven took a walk together. Everywhere they went men and women saluted them, pointed them out, and bowed. Goethe exclaimed, "Isn't it maddening! I simply can't escape this homage."

Beethoven replied, "Don't be too much distressed by it; it is just possible that some of it may be for me."

CANDIDATES

☐ A seminary student who finally had a chance to candidate for a church gave them his best sermon. They promised to let him know after a meeting the following week to discuss a call. He was the only candidate being considered.

A long week followed, but no letter from the church. A month went by, then several months. A few years later when he was preaching nearby, a lady approached him after the service. She was the clerk of the church which had considered him. Curious as to why he hadn't received a call, he asked the reason.

"Oh, they did vote to call you," she replied. "I was the church clerk, but when they instructed me to write you, I began to wonder what my husband would think of my writing to a strange man, so I never did let you know."

☐ A Welsh preacher was candidating in an English church. In the sermon he said, "This verse in Galatians goes like this in the original." Then he talked in Welsh, which sounded very cultured to the congregation. He saw a man on the back seat laughing as though his sides would split. Continuing in Welsh he said, "Thou jolly old Welshman, I pray thee, do not give me away."

☐ A young man just out of seminary was candidating at a church. In a meeting with the pulpit committee later that day, the candidate was questioned by one of its members, an English teacher in the local high school. "Young man, when you speak in public it's important to use good English. Bad grammar might drive people away.

Which would you say was proper—to speak of a hen as sitting or setting on the eggs?"

The young preacher thought a moment, then responded. "It's like back on the farm. When the hen did some cackling, we would have to decide whether she was laying or lying!"

CHILDREN

☐ A six-year-old boy went to a luncheon. During the meal he was seated next to the hostess, who noticed he was having a little difficulty cutting his steak. "Give me your knife and I'll help you cut your meat," she offered.

He replied, "Oh, don't bother. We have tough steak like this at home lots of times."

☐ A fifth-grader wrote an essay on going to the moon. He ended, "After going to the moon, my big ambition is to travel a lot!"

☐ A boy had an oversized Saint Bernard dog on a leash. A passer-by asked the boy where he was taking the dog.

Said the boy, "I don't know. I'm waiting to see where he's going first."

☐ A mother, trying to teach her son not to be afraid of thunder, told him it was the angels bowling. One night during a severe storm she found him sitting up in bed. "Why are you frightened?" she asked.

He replied, "I don't mind as long as the angels bowl; but when they stop and clap, that's what I don't like."

☐ "Some plants," said the teacher, "have the prefix 'dog.' For instance, there is the dog rose, the dogwood, the dog violet. Now who can name another plant prefixed by 'dog'?"

"I can," shouted a redhead from the back how. "Collieflower."

☐ A mother was teaching her child to pray. When he got to the part, "I surrender everything to Thee, everything I own," he abruptly broke off and whispered to himself, "except my baby rabbit."

☐ Mother was trying to get nine-year-old Joan to study her Sunday school lesson. At length mother took her own Bible from the dresser.

"All right, mother," said Joan, "but let's study out of grandfather's Bible. It's much more interesting than yours."

"Oh, no, Joan. They're exactly alike."

"Well, I think grandfather's must be more interesting than yours. He reads it so much more."

☐ When Mark Twain was traveling with his family in Europe, it turned out to be a triumphal tour, for practically every ruler of a nation invited them to dine with him. Once, on receiving an invitation from the emperor of Germany, his little girl said, "Father, you will soon know everybody except God."

☐ A little fellow's cousins had been visiting. When they left, he began crying.

When asked why he replied, "Now I have no one to fight with!"

☐ A little girl got out of the wrong side of bed one morning, ugly and naughty as she could be. Her mother punished her. At breakfast she came down all smiling to the table, happy like her own lovely self. Said her father, "I'm glad that little girl I met earlier this morning didn't stay to breakfast. My, she was cross and naughty. I'm glad instead we have this lovely girl."

She sat up in her chair straight and said, "Daddy, I'm still here!"

☐ A five-year-old, given a lemon lollypop, shoved it aside after giving it one thoughtful lick. "This one's green; it'll taste better when it gets ripe."

☐ Johnnie was gazing at his baby brother, who lay squealing and wailing in his crib. "Has he come from heaven?" asked Johnnie.

"Yes, dear."

"No wonder they put him out."

☐ Before leaving for dinner at a friend's house, David's mother coached him to be sure to compliment the hostess on the meal.

After dinner, nudged by his mother, he looked at the hostess and exclaimed, "That sure was a swell meal—what there was of it!"

☐ Little Johnny's mother had just presented the family with twins. The household was in a state of excitement.

Father said to Johnny, "If you'll tell your teacher, I'm sure she'll give you a day off."

That afternoon Johnny came home from school radiant. "I don't have to go to school tomorrow," he proudly announced.

"Did you tell your teacher about the twins?" his father asked.

"No, I just told her I had a baby sister. I'm saving the other one for next week."

☐ Two little nine-year-old girls were comparing bedtimes. "I stay up till nine o'clock," said the first.

"Oh," replied the second, "I have to go to bed at eight o'clock. My mother is an hour meaner than yours."

☐ A teacher asked his class to make a sentence using the word *influenza*.

One of the boys responded, "He opened the window and in-flu-enza."

☐ Back home after morning church, where he had misbehaved, little John was told that as punishment he would have to eat dinner by himself. So his mother set up a small table not far from the large dining table. The father thought he would ask Johnny to pray. Johnny said, "Thank you, Lord, for preparing a table before me in the presence of my enemies."

CHILDREN IN CHURCH

☐ The ushers were passing the offering plate. It was one little fellow's first time in church. As they neared him, he leaned over to his father, "Don't pay for me, daddy. I'm under five." (Used by permission of *Pageant,* April 1958)

☐ A preacher was invited to deliver a sermon at a country church on a week night. He took his little boy with him. As they entered the church they noticed a box marked, "For the preacher." The minister dropped a dollar in the box. When the sermon was over, the deacons opened the box to count the money and out rolled the dollar bill. They handed it to the preacher, whereupon his little boy exclaimed, "Daddy, if you had put more into it, you would have gotten more out of it!"

☐ A preacher, seeing a sobbing boy outside the church door, asked, "What's the matter?"

"I don't have any money, and I want to go into church," wept the lad.

The preacher gave him a dime. After the service the boy passed the preacher at the door. "Hey, mister, here's your dime. I didn't have to pay to get in after all."

☐ Just before church a father gave his little girl two coins: a nickel and a quarter. "Now, Marie, put one coin in the offering, whichever you choose." Father was trying to develop Marie's unselfishness.

After church, father asked which coin Marie had given. She explained, "Just before the plate came round the minister said, 'The Lord loveth a cheerful giver,' and I knew I could give the nickel a lot more cheerfully than the quarter, so I gave it."

☐ A five-year-old attended a Sunday evening service for the first time. Later, when he knelt beside his bed to say his prayers, he said, "Dear Lord, we had such a good time at church tonight. I wish You could have been there."

☐ When the plate went by a little girl during her first time in church, she dropped her penny in like mother told her. Then she asked, "What will come out of the plate, bubble gum or licorice stick?"

☐ When on the Sunday before Memorial Day the church organ prelude suddenly blared out the strains of the National Anthem, little Joe, a lover of sports, whispered loudly, "Who's playing today, dad?"

☐ A little girl was taken to church for her first time. When everyone knelt, she asked, "What are they going to do?"
The mother whispered, "Sssh, they are going to say their prayers."
Amazed, the child looked up, "What—with all their clothes on?"

CHILDREN'S DAY

☐ A little girl was visiting her aunt on Children's Day. "I have a gift for you," said auntie. "You may take your choice."
She had placed on the table a dime and a dollar. The little girl replied, "Mother always taught me to take the smaller, so I'll take this." She reached for the dime. Then she added, "Just so I don't lose the dime, I'll wrap it up in this piece of green paper."

☐ On Children's Day a little girl said to her mother, "Where's my present?"
"Why?" asked mother.
The answer was, "On Mother's Day I got you something. On Father's Day I'll give him the present I bought yesterday. Now it's Children's Day; what did you get me?"

☐ A little girl, just back from Children's Day service where she had heard a talk on "Letting your light shine," asked her mother what "shine" meant.

Her mother explained, "It means being good, kind, obedient, and cheerful."

That afternoon the little girl after being naughty excused herself, "I've blowed myself out."

CHOIR

☐ The boys' choir was making its usual Sunday morning processional. As was customary, the first boy in the procession carried a banner. When the congregation looked in his direction their eyes nearly popped out. Instead of the usual symbols were some words. They read, "We want more pay!"

☐ An aspiring choir soloist was vocalizing in her living room. The windows were open and a handyman was working on the lawn nearby. Seeing him, she asked, "How do you like my execution?"

He looked up. "I'm in favor of it."

☐ A fellow hoping to sing in the choir took singing lessons. Some weeks later his teacher made this comment, "I play the white keys and I play the black keys, but you sing in the cracks."

☐ A minister noted for his efficiency operated a small farm on the side. Observing the hired man sitting idly by the plow as the horses took a needed rest, and recalling that he was paying the man twenty-five cents an hour, he gently said, "Wouldn't it be a good plan for you to have a pair of shears and trim the bushes while the horses are resting?"

"I'll be glad to, your reverence," came the reply, "if you'll take a peck of potatoes into the pulpit and peel them during the choir anthem."

☐ The benediction had just been pronounced ending the Sunday morning service in a Canadian church. The choir started its recessional, singing as they marched in perfect step down the center aisle to the back of the church. The last lady was wearing shoes with very slender heels. Without a thought for her fancy heels, she marched toward the grating that covered the hot air register in the middle of the aisle. Suddenly the heel of one shoe sank into the hole in the register grate. In a flash she realized her predicament. Not wishing to hold up the whole recessional while she stepped back to yank out her heel, she did the next best thing. Without missing a step she slipped her foot out of her shoe and continued marching down the aisle. There wasn't a hitch. The recessional moved with clocklike precision.

The first man after her spotted the situation and without losing a step, reached down and pulled up her shoe. But the entire grate came with it. Surprised, but still singing, the man kept on going down the aisle, holding in his hand the grate with the shoe attached. Everything still moved like clockwork. Still in tune and still in step, the next man stepped into the open register.

☐ Bulletin item: "The newly organized senior choir will sing for the first time at the morning service, and a real threat is anticipated."

☐ Asked what her mother did, a little girl, just remembering her mother had joined the choir the week before, blurted out, "She's a chorus girl."

☐ "What do you think of my composition?" a youthful choir member, who was an aspiring composer, asked of the organist who had looked them over.

"They will be played when Beethoven and Bach are forgotten," replied the organist.

"Really?"

"Yes, but not before."

☐ A college girl who sang solos in the choir of one of the local churches received an anonymous letter which praised her singing and announced that her unknown admirer would sit in the balcony the next Sunday morning, wearing a white chrysanthemum in his lapel. That night on a date with a member of the football team she couldn't resist telling him, then forgot the matter.

Sunday morning, just before time for her solo she remembered the note. Looking toward the balcony, she couldn't see the people without standing up. As she waited, her imagination ran away with her. Would he be tall, dark, and handsome? Mysterious? Then the notes of the organ began playing the prelude to her song. Excitedly, she almost jumped up, then almost collapsed with embarrassment. Grinning at her from the balcony was the entire football squad, each with a white chrysanthemum in his buttonhole.

☐ Church bulletin: "The high school choir has been disbanded for the summer with the thanks of the church."

☐ Choir leader: Don't forget, choir, the sopranos will sing until we get to the River Jordan. Then when they reach the River Jordan, the rest of you will come in.

☐ A soloist was asked if he ever liked to get paid for singing. His reply: "Doesn't the musical scale begin and end with *dough?*"

CHRISTMAS

☐ The day before Christmas was a hectic one. Father was worried with bundles and burdens. Mother's nerves reached the breaking point more than once. The little girl seemed to be in the way wherever she went. Finally, she was hustled up to bed. As she knelt to pray, the feverish excitement so mixed her up, she said, "Forgive us our Christmases, as we forgive those who Christmas against us."

☐ On the Sunday before Christmas a church bulletin read: "Our adult choir will sing, 'I Heard the Bills on Christmas Day.' "

☐ "You're not kidding when you say you are engaged to four different boys at once?"

"Yes, it's true. I can hardly wait till after Christmas to straighten things out."

☐ A mother took her little girl to see the department store Santa Claus. Santa gave the child an apple.

"What do you say to Santa Claus?" said the mother.

The little girl replied, "Peel it!"

☐ "Now, class," said the teacher to her second grade class, "let's get to work and make this the best Christmas ever."

"But, teacher," said one small tot, "I don't see how we can improve on the first one."

☐ A few days before Christmas two ladies stood looking into a department store window at a large display of the manger scene with clay figures of the baby Jesus, Mary, Joseph, the shepherds, the wise men, and the animals. Disgustedly one said, "Look at that. The church trying to horn in on Christmas!"

☐ A business man who parked his car in the same lot when he went to business every day found a greeting card on his front seat ten days before Christmas. He was pleased that the parking attendant would be so thoughtful. A week later he found another card on the front seat. It simply said, "Second notice."

☐ For Christmas a husband wanted a car. His wife wanted a fur coat. They got a fur coat and kept it in the garage.

☐ Wife to husband: This year let's give each other more practical gifts like socks and fur coats.

☐ During the Christmas season a man went to church, and just before the pastoral prayer raised his hand. "I've got a problem," he told the minister. "I want you to pray for me, especially at this time of year."

The minister asked, "What's your problem?"

He answered, "I'm a spendthrift and my wife is a spendthrift. We throw money around as though we were drunken sailors."

The minister said, "All right, we'll remember you in prayer right after the offering."

☐ Q.: What are among Santa Claus's best-known exclamations?
A.: Ho! Ho! Ho!
Q.: Can you think of any others?
A: Owe! Owe! Owe!

CHURCH

☐ Little girl, visiting friend's church: Why do you have two pulpits —one on one side, and one on the other side?

Little friend: The minister reads the Bible from one pulpit, and he preaches from the other.

Little girl: Why is that?

Friend: I don't know, unless it's to show that what he preaches is far removed from the Bible.

☐ One church's Sunday morning order of service always included the reading of the twenty-third Psalm. One week a visitor with a shrill voice moved several words ahead of the congregation. At the end of the reading a husband whispered to his wife, "Who is that lady who was by the still waters while everybody else was lying down in green pastures?"

☐ A minister was going over the church rolls with his board. After many of the names were these initials: FBPO.

After a while the board members said, "Please explain the meaning of these initials."

The pastor answered, "They mean 'For Burial Purposes Only.'"

☐ An old preacher reported a big revival in his church. Someone asked him how many had been added to the membership.

He replied, "We did not add any, but we dropped a hundred."

☐ A visitor remarked to an old friend that in heaven there would be no partings.

The friend replied tartly, "What I hoped for was a place with no meetings."

☐ A man had been looking for a church to attend, and he happened into a small one in which the congregation was reading with the minister. They were repeating, "We have left undone those things which we ought to have done and we have done those things which we ought not to have done."

The man dropped into a seat and sighed with relief, "I've found my crowd at last."

☐ A geologist studying the strata of rock under Saint Paul's Cathedral in London reported that Saint Paul's was moving down Fleet Street at the rate of one inch a thousand years. Someone commented, "The church ought to move faster than that!"

☐ In a church where everybody sat toward the rear, a stranger walked in and took a front seat. After the service, the minister greeted the stranger and asked why he sat up front.

"I'm a bus driver," he volunteered, "and I came to learn how you succeed in getting people to move to the back."

CHURCH ATTENDANCE

☐ The pastor of a small church was asked if he ever feared his congregation.

His reply, "Oh, no. The choir and I usually have them outnumbered!"

☐ This classified ad appeared in a midwestern newspaper: "Wanted! Men, women, boys, and girls to sit in slightly used pews this Sunday morning and night."

☐ A bright but cynical young man called one Monday morning on an elderly lady who always went to church. "Good morning," he said, "and how are you today?" Then he asked, "You were at church yesterday, no doubt?"

"Oh, yes, I was—morning and evening."

"I didn't go," confessed the young man; "but what was the preacher's text?"

After thinking a while the lady replied, "I'm sorry, but I can't remember. I know it was a good sermon, though."

"But you do know what the sermon was about at the evening service?" asked the lad.

"No, I can't say that I do. It seems to have slipped my mind, too."

The young man smiled. "That's queer. What's the use of going to church if you can't remember the preacher's sermon?"

The elderly lady looked at the young man. "Lad," she asked, "will you do me a favor? Take this old clothes basket to the well and bring it back full of water."

"Come, come," said the young man, "I'm not quite so stupid as that. You know there wouldn't be a drop of water in that basket when I got back. It's a wicker basket. It's not solid throughout. It wouldn't hold water."

It was the old lady's turn to smile. "Perhaps you are right. I dare say there wouldn't be any water it in, but the basket would be a bit cleaner."

☐ A questionnaire mailed out by a church asked, "How far do you live from the church?" and "How long does it take you to get to church?" One member answered, "I live about four blocks from the church, and to get there it takes me about three months."

☐ A man who attended the morning church service never came at night. One day the preacher asked him why. "I simply can't digest more than one sermon a day."

Suggested the preacher, "I rather think the fault is not with your digestion, but with your appetite."

☐ 1st lady: Our Sunday evening attendance is so low that we often have only fifteen or twenty there.

2nd lady: That's nothing. It's so bad in our church some Sunday nights that when the minister says, "Dearly beloved," it sounds like a proposal.

☐ A church held two identical morning services. One Sunday the pastor noticed a parishioner arrive very late during the 9:30 A.M. service. To his surprise the parishioner was in his seat when the 11 o'clock service began. But when the congregation rose to sing the hymn before the sermon, he left, explaining to the usher, "This is where I came in!"

☐ A church and a night club were situated a block apart. A parrot, part of the night club act, lived in the rafters of the club. One Saturday night the club had a fire, forcing the parrot to seek shelter elsewhere. Noting a high beam near the ceiling of the church, he roosted there for the night. Sunday morning he was awakened by a crowd of people entering the church. Looking down at the pastor, he chirped, "That's a new master of ceremonies."

Spotting the choir, he remarked, "New chorus girls."

Then gazing out on the congregation, he crowed, "Same old crowd!"

☐ One day the telephone rang in the office of the church in Washington where the late President Roosevelt used to attend. An eager voice asked, "Tell me, do you expect the president to attend church this Sunday?"

"That," the minister replied, "I cannot promise. But we do expect the Lord to be here, and we expect that will be incentive enough for a reasonably large attendance."

☐ Question: Why is a church like a convention?
Answer: Because so many families send just one delegate.

CHURCH DINNERS

☐ A circular letter to the Men's Fellowship read, "All members are requested to bring their wives and one other covered dish, to the annual banquet."

☐ Young bride as she brings a dish for the social: The two things I prepare best are meatballs and peach pie.

Young man standing near: And which one is this?

☐ Guest (at a church social): Look here, waiter, I ordered chicken pie; but there isn't a single piece of chicken in it.

Waiter: That's not strange. We also have cottage cheese, but so far as I know there's not a cottage in it.

☐ A family had enjoyed the church social, but weren't able to finish all the food served them. The father signaled a waitress. "May we have a bag for the extra, please. We'll take it home to the dog."

"Oh, great," piped up his little daughter. "Are we going to get a dog?"

☐ To his embarrassment a guest preacher discovered just before being called on to speak that his upper plate had cracked. "I'm afraid I'll have to cancel my sermon," said the preacher to the chairman.

"No need to cancel it," came the reply. "Here's a spare upper I have in my pocket."

The guest minister tried it, but it didn't fit. The chairman, quick as a flash, produced another, then another, till a fourth one fitted exactly. When the preacher finished his well-received talk, he said to the chairman, "How happy I am that you happen to be a dentist."

"Dentist not at all," said the chairman. "I'm an undertaker."

CHURCH LIBRARY

☐ Librarian (to the pastor): Please do me a favor and ask that new convert to call me "librarian" and not "bookie."

COLLECTIONS

☐ An unemployed preacher with a good physical build wanted to join the police force. The police commissioner interviewed him, expressed satisfaction at his physical condition, then asked some routine questions, among them, "What would you do to break up a rioting mob?"

The minister thought a minute, then answered, "I'd take up a collection!"

☐ Little Mary was given two nickels, one for Sunday school and one for candy. On the way to Sunday school one of the nickels rolled down a sewer and disappeared. Exclaimed Mary, "Oh, my, there goes the Lord's nickel."

☐ Three tightwads went late to a service to avoid the offering. To their dismay they learned it was to be taken up at the end. But they solved the problem. One fainted, and the other two carried him out.

☐ A man entered a candy store one Sunday morning and asked the man behind the counter to change a dime. As the clerk gave the man two nickels, he commented, "I hope you enjoy the sermon."

☐ To get money for a much-needed new building, a minister asked all who would give fifty dollars to stand. Then he immediately turned to his youth orchestra and told them to play "The Star-Spangled Banner."

Next week he had another scheme. On Saturday, he had the sexton wire the church so that every seat had a little button on it which was connected with a central switch on the pulpit. One press on the pulpit switch would send a current of electrical juice to every seat. On Sunday at the end of the service he asked all who would give fifty dollars to stand. No one got up. Then he pushed the switch. Everyone jumped up. Monday when he was cleaning through the church, the sexton found two electrocuted Scotchmen lying in the seats.

☐ A breathless silence fell over the congregation. The church was jammed to the doors. The back balcony was crowded. A special offering had been taken and the total given was to be announced at the end of the service. The goal was twenty thousand dollars. The ushers had finished counting it and brought a note with the total written on it to the pastor. Now was the climactic moment. "The total amount received was . . . ," the pastor began; then his forehead clouded over as he hesitantly read, "twenty thousand dollars and three cents." Pausing a moment, he said, "That's a strange total. Twenty thousand dollars and three cents. Three cents! There must be a Scotchman here."

From the balcony came a voice, "Hoot mon, there are three of us here."

☐ Someone asked a man how much he was going to give to a church offering.

He said, "I guess I can give ten dollars and not feel it."

"Brother," said the first man, "make it twenty and feel it."

☐ Three ministers in northern Indiana were discussing their problems because three railroads converged in their town. One said, "My church is too close to the New York Central. When the long freight comes crashing through during my service every Sunday morning, it's difficult for the congregation to hear the preaching."

A second minister explained, "My church is so close to the Pennsylvania tracks that when the big diesel with its long passenger train comes whistling through, we can't hear the choir singing."

The third minister complained, "My trouble is that *Nickel Plate*. It comes right down my middle aisle at offering time every Sunday morning."

☐ When it came offering time in a church service, a lady began to fumble in her purse. When it seemed she wouldn't come up with any money, a little boy behind her exclaimed, "Here's my dime, madam. I'll climb under the seat."

☐ When a special offering was taken for work in the Kentucky mountains, a prankster dropped a button into the plate. Later the preacher announced: "Some put dollars in; some put quarters; some put dimes; some put nickels; some put cents; and those who had no sense put buttons!"

☐ Home after the morning service, the family began to criticize. Father thought the sermon was too long. Mother felt the choir was punk. Sister didn't like the "shrieking" soloist. But they all quieted down when little brother chirped out, "I don't think it was a bad show at all for a dime!"

☐ When the collection plate was passed to Mr. Dives during a special missionary offering, he shook his head and whispered to the usher, "I never give to missions."

"Then take something out of the plate," the usher whispered back. "The money is for the heathen."

☐ Sister Smith confided to the pastor, "My husband's purse is made of pigskin."

"What do you mean?" asked the pastor.

"Every time he opens it for an offering, it squeals."

☐ A Sunday school teacher was trying to explain the difference between a collection and an offering. He told about a boy whose mother served a chicken dinner. The boy sneaked some good meat on a plate for his dog—first a leg, then a wing, then some white meat. His mother spotted it. "Oh, no, you don't!" She made the boy put back the meat and after the meal gave him a dish of bones for Towser. As the boy put them down in front of the dog, he apologized, "I did have an offering for you. Now it's only a collection!"

☐ "When I look at my congregation," said one preacher, "I ask myself, 'Where are the poor?' And then when I look at the offering plate, I say to myself, 'Where are the rich?' "

☐ A church was having difficulty in getting money from its members to pay for the mortgage on its new Sunday school building, even though the folks kept informing the pastor they were praying for the completion of the structure. So one Sunday morning the offering suddenly skyrocketed when this slogan appeared on all collection plates, "Pay now, pray later."

COMMITTEES

☐ A boy saw a giraffe for the first time. Home from the zoo, he described it to his father. "It has the face of a deer, the neck of an ostrich, front legs like a camel, and back legs like a horse."

The father replied, "There's no such animal." Then one day the boy took his father to the zoo for *his* first look at a giraffe. After a few puzzling moments, the father commented, "Must be the work of a committee."

☐ Definition of a committee: The unwilling, conscripted from the unqualified to do the unnecessary.

☐ 1st person: Why are the Ten Commandments so brief and concise?
2nd person: They didn't come through a committee.

COMPLAINING

☐ A man drowning in deep water began to holler for help. "I can't swim," he shouted over and over.
From the shore came the response, "Neither can I, but I'm not hollering about it."

☐ In a lumber camp nobody wanted to be the cook because the men were so insulting about the food. When the lumberjacks sat down to eat, one would call out, "What kind of soup is this? It tastes like kerosene. Is it bean soup?"
And someone else would shout, "No, the bean soup tastes like turpentine."
Since no one volunteered to take the cooking job, the foreman decided to appoint someone. He said, "Joe, you be the next cook." When Joe began to protest, the foreman said, "Now wait just a minute. Let me finish. You'll be the cook, but the first person who finds fault will have to take over the cooking job."
Perhaps the foreman shouldn't have told the whole group of lumberjacks about this rule; for no one complained for a whole week, then a month, then two months. After three months had gone by, Joe was so sick and tired of cooking that he thought he would force them to complain by emptying the big salt container into the soup. He stirred it, put the soup on the table, then shouted, "Come and get it!"
The first fellow who took a spoonful yelled, "Boy, is that soup salty," but remembering what he had just said, he sputtered quickly, "but this is just the way I like it!"

☐ The village pessimist, no matter what, used always to find something to complain about. For several years the crops had been poor. But one year, there was a magnificent harvest. The potatoes were big and mealy. The townsfolk felt that now, at last, the pessimist would be unable to complain. Someone asked what he thought of the fine potato crop.

Looking around at the rich harvest, he said peevishly, "But where are the little ones to feed the pigs?"

COMPUTERS

☐ A man received a computerized bill in the mail for the amount of zero dollars and zero cents. He sent it back with a notation that since he owed nothing, he should not receive a bill. Next month came another bill. Again the amount was zero dollars and zero cents. When it happened a third time, he sent them a check in the amount of zero dollars and zero cents. Back came a computerized note, "Paid in full."

☐ A young man wishing to get advice on what occupation he was best fitted for, went to a service that used computers in their counseling. As he answered their questions, they fed the information into the computer, then eagerly waited its verdict. Out came the answer: "Motherhood."

CONTENTMENT

☐ A farmer known for his frugality, visiting a new shopping center for the first time, was asked what he thought of it. He replied, "I don't know when I have seen so many things I could do without."

☐ A man was given an attic room in a poor home down south, which the hostess of the home kindly opened to him.

At night the hostess came up with a light and said, "We're very glad to have you here as our guest. We're sorry we don't have better quarters for you. If there is anything you want and we don't have it, we'll show you how to get along without it."

COURTSHIP

☐ A charming belle was being courted by a young banker. When queried by a friend, she said flatly, "Doesn't mean a thing. If that stuffed shirt proposes, I'll give him a deaf ear."

Next week she was wearing the young banker's large diamond. Said the friend, "I thought you said you'd be deaf to any proposal from him?"

"I did," replied the belle, looking at the lovely diamond, "but I didn't say I'd be stone deaf."

☐ A young fellow slipped quietly into a jeweler's store. He handed the jeweler a ring. "I would like some names engraved on it."

"What names do you want?"

"From James to Barbara," the young man embarrassingly whispered.

"Please take some advice from me," said the jeweler as he looked up from the ring. "Have it just engraved, 'From James.'"

☐ A girl and boy fell madly in love at first sight. He saw her every day. When a new job sent the boy to a distant city, so deeply in love was he that he telegraphed a message of devotion every morning. So every morning for three years the same Western Union messenger boy knocked on the girl's door. At the end of three years they were married—the girl and the Western Union boy.

☐ Two big tears were floating down the river of time. They began to engage in conversation. Said the first tear, "I am the tear of the girl who lost her boyfriend to another girl." "Don't feel so badly," consoled the other tear. "I'm the tear of the girl who got him."

☐ The police chief in a Missouri city received a letter from a woman in another state who asked him to find her a perfect man. She wanted to marry him. Her specifications: a man about sixty with no children, preferably a railroad executive, banker, or lawyer. The chief of police sent the letter to the Bureau of Missing Persons.

☐ 1st girl: I hear he proposed and you accepted. Did he tell you that he had proposed to me first?

2nd girl: No, but he did mention that he had done a lot of foolish things before we met.

☐ A farmer, making his nightly rounds, saw a figure standing near the barn, holding a lantern.

"Who are you?" the farmer hollered.

"It's only me, Clarence," the neighbor boy answered with a giggle.

"And what are you doing here so late?" the farmer demanded.

"I'm courting your daughter Sarah."

"But why the lantern?" the farmer inquired. "When I was courting my missus, I didn't take a lantern!"

"Yes, sir," Clarence solemnly answered, "Anybody can see that."

☐ She: Do you remember the night you proposed to me?

He: Yes.

She: I was silent for a whole hour after.

He: That was the happiest hour of my life.

☐ The young boyfriend explained to his girl friend's mother why he had rung the doorbell. "Excuse me for coming to the door to get your daughter, but my horn isn't working."

☐ Jim: Yep, the engagement's off—she won't marry me.

Joe: How come? Didn't you tell her about your rich uncle?

Jim: Sure did—now she's my aunt!

☐ He thought it safer to write to the girl's father asking her hand in marriage. Though an ardent lover, he was a poor speller. His note ran, "I want your daughter—the flour of your family."

"The flour of my family is good," responded the father, "but are you sure it isn't my dough you're after?"

☐ After a long engagement had been broken, the young man was handed a package from the postman containing all the letters he had written his ex-fiancée. It was marked, "Fourth Class Male."

☐ A rich retired bachelor, making out his will, told his lawyer, "I wish my estate divided equally among four ladies. Each of them refused my proposal of marriage years ago. To their refusal I owe all my earthly happiness."

☐ Girl to friends: No, he hasn't sprung the question yet, but his voice sure has an engagement ring in it.

☐ An anxious girl was taken by her steady, though noncommittal, boyfriend to a restaurant. When she asked the waiter if she could have rice instead of potatoes, her boyfriend said, "Sure, do you wish it boiled or fried?"

Quick as a flash her answer came, "I'd like mine tossed."

DEACONS

☐ A young man was driving a deacon to a service in the next town. The youthful driver had his streamlined chariot hitting seventy miles an hour. The deacon leaned over, "Aren't we going a little too fast?"

"Oh, don't you believe in a guardian angel, deacon? He'll take care of us."

"Yes," the deacon replied. "He would if he were here, but I'm afraid we left him miles back!"

41

☐ First preacher: How many deacons do you have?

Second preacher: Sixteen.

First preacher: Are they all active?

Second preacher: Yes, all of them; eight are for me, and eight against.

☐ Deacon: My wife dreamed last night she was married to a millionnaire.

Trustee: Don't feel bad. Mine thinks that in the daytime.

☐ A milkman who delivered his route by horse and wagon used to give the same testimony at every prayer meeting. It was the same old sentence, "I'm not making much progress, but praise the Lord, I'm established." One April morning when he was on his route, his wagon sank into deep mud and his horse could not budge it. Along came a deacon who could never quite accept the milkman's testimony. Looking the situation over he said with a smile, "Well, Brother, I see you're not making much progress, but you're sure established!"

☐ Member (to pastor): Why don't you ever have Deacon Smith pray before your sermon?

Pastor: What—and have him say, "Now I lay me down to sleep?"

☐ A lady asked a photographer to make a large picture from a snapshot of her deceased husband, who had been an esteemed deacon for many years. She wanted it touched up. First, she asked if he could curl his moustache. The photographer replied that he thought he could. Then she asked if the wart on his chin could be removed. He thought he could do that. Then she said, "Could you remove his hat and show his curly hair?" Again the photographer acquiesced. "Yes, that can be done, but on which side did he part his hair?"

She answered, "You'll find that out when you take off his hat!"

☐ Prayer meeting was almost over. The pastor thought he would ask a member of the official board to close in prayer. "Deacon Jones, will you please lead?"

Silence. Deacon Jones had fallen asleep. His wife nudged him just as the pastor repeated his request. "Deacon Jones, will you please lead?"

"Lead," stammered the confused deacon, "I just dealt."

DENOMINATIONS

☐ One Monday a little boy said to his pal, "Yesterday I went to the Baptist church. What abomination do you belong to?"

☐ Six men were marooned on an island: two Jews, two Catholics, and two Baptists.

The two Jews started the Temple Emanuel.

The two Catholics started the Church of the Holy Name.

The two Baptists started the First Baptist Church and the Second Baptist Church.

☐ In a city-wide revival meeting the presiding preacher, an enthusiastic Southern Baptist, asked the congregation, "How many of you are Southern Baptists? Please stand."

One of the few who failed to rise was a little old lady near the front. "Lady, what are you?" asked the leader.

"I'm a Presbyterian," she meekly answered.

"Why are you a Presbyterian?" continued the leader.

"Well," replied the little old lady hesitatingly, "my grandfather was a Presbyterian, my father was a Presbyterian, and my husband was a Presbyterian."

"Suppose," roared the leader, "that your grandfather and father and all your relatives had been morons; what would that have made you?"

"Oh, I see," she said thoughtfully, "I would have been a Southern Baptist."

☐ The registrar in an undenominational seminary noted that in the incoming freshman class a good percentage had signed up indicating church preference. Presbyterian, Baptist, Lutheran, Methodist were all represented in normal ratio. But he came across one card signed by a young man who had majored in architecture in his undergraduate work. He put down "Gothic."

☐ "Are you in the army of the Lord?"
"I surely am."
"What department?"
"I'm a Baptist."
"You aren't in the army. You're in the navy."

☐ A Baptist was comparing her church with several other churches. "When it comes to dignity, we can't be compared to the Episcopalians," she said. "As for ritual, the Lutherans have it all over us, and in regard to singing, the Nazarenes have us beat."
Then she added, "But when it comes to humility, we're tops!"

☐ A Presbyterian minister, surprised when three Episcopalian vestrymen whom he had met on the golf course walked into church, whispered to an usher, "Get three chairs for the Episcopalians." The usher didn't quite understand, so the pastor repeated, "Give three chairs to the Episcopalians."
The usher, a little puzzled, stepped to the front, and in pep-leader stance yelled to an amazed congregation, "Ready, everybody! All together! Let's give three cheers for the Episcopalians!"

☐ Two ministers, each convinced of his own denomination's superiority, were engaged in good-natured conversation. "Who's to really say who is the better," commented one. "After all, we both do the Lord's work."
"Yes," said the other with a twinkle in his eye. "You do it in your way, and I in His."

☐ A little girl was naming the various denominations to which her relatives belonged. "Baptists, Lutherans, Presbyterians, Seventh-day Adventists." Then she said, "Why I have an aunt and uncle that I think—yes, I'm sure of it—that for some time were six-day atheists!"

☐ A stranger in town asked, "Where will I find a Presbyterian church?"

"Go down to the corner and you will find the United Presbyterian Church. That's not it. Go one more block and on the next corner you will find the Reformed Presbyterian Church. That's not it. One block further there's a church that's neither United nor Reformed. That's it."

☐ A Presbyterian family had a death while their minister was away. When the local Methodist minister was asked to conduct the funeral service, he said he would have to clear it with his bishop. Back came the bishop's telegram, "Sure, bury all the Presbyterians you can!"

☐ A Presbyterian elder advertised his car for sale. A Baptist deacon answered the ad. "How do I know it runs as well as you claim?" asked the Baptist deacon.

"You can trust my word. I'm a Presbyterian elder."

"I'll take it," replied the other. "I'll drive it home and send you the money in the mail. You can trust me, for I'm a Baptist deacon."

When the elder arrived home he asked his wife, "What's a Baptist deacon?"

"Oh," came the answer, "a Baptist deacon is about the same as a Presbyterian elder."

"Oh, no," groaned the elder, "I've lost my car."

☐ Two denominations could not agree whether to say, "Forgive us our debts" or "Forgive us our trespasses." So the newspaper reported that the Presbyterians went back to their "trespasses" while the Methodists went back to their "debts."

☐ Three churches, all different denominations, were located on the same main intersection. One Sunday morning a passerby heard the first church singing, "Will There Be Any Stars in My Crown?"

The next church was singing, "No, Not One."

From the third church came, "Oh, That Will Be Glory for Me."

☐ The masked bandit lined up all the customers in the small store against the wall, then went from one to the other, demanding their money.

Finally he reached the last man who said, "You wouldn't rob a minister, would you?"

"What church do you preach in?" the bandit asked.

"I'm a Baptist."

Placing his gun in his left hand, the bandit stuck out his right hand, "Put it there, brother; I'm a Baptist, too."

☐ 1st boy: Does your church have any big guns?

2nd boy: No, but our cathedral does have a canon.

☐ One Christmastime the decoration committee of the local Baptist church was trying to decide where to put a large Christmas tree. The best suggestion was the baptistry, located at the front of the church to the right of the pulpit.

Thereafter the young people referred to the Christmas tree as the "baptist-tree."

☐ A lady whose husband's climb up the ladder of business led her to a more ritzy way of life changed to a better car, better home, better furs, and a better church. After another major advance which landed her in the Cadillac stage, she paid a visit to her latest minister. "I've had the feeling for some time that I should join with my friends at the Saint Ritz church," she said, swinging her furs around her back and flashing her two carat diamonds. "What would be your opinion, sir?"

"My dear lady," the clergyman replied, "it matters little what kind of label you put on an empty bottle!"

DISCIPLINE OF CHILDREN

☐ Two fathers were discussing the problems of raising families. One asked, "Do you strike your children?"
"Only in self-defense," came the answer.

☐ A mother was trying to explain the meaning of grandfather and grandmother.
"Now if grandfather is my father can you tell me who grandmother is?"
"Sure," replied the little girl. "Grandmother is the white-haired lady who keeps you from spanking me."

☐ A lively little fellow climbed on a hobby horse in the toy section of a big department store. When his mother told him to get off, he stubbornly refused. Her arms were full of packages, so she tried to bribe him with promises of candy and gum, but no success. The boy just shook his head no and rocked back and forth. Then the store Santa Claus noticed the embarrassed mother's plight. He bent over and whispered something in the boy's ears. Like a shot he was off the horse and out of the store, his mother right behind. A surprised salesman asked, "What under the sun did you promise the boy?"
"Promise him?" asked the disgusted Santa. "I promised him nothing. I told him to get off or I'd kick him out of his trousers!"

☐ A little boy was picking up his toys and tidying his room. His playmate said, "Oh, I see you're picking up your toys and straightening your room. I suppose your mother is going to give you something if you clean it all up nice."
"Oh, no," retorted the boy, "she's going to give me something if I don't clean things up."

☐ The department store was crowded with shoppers. A young mother had the added difficulty of a small daughter pulling and tugging at her side, and whimpering incessantly. Suddenly the harassed mother pleaded softly, "Quiet, Susanna, just calm yourself and take it easy." An admiring clerk commented on the mother's psychology, then turned to the child, "So your name is Susanna."

"Oh, no," interrupted the mother. "Her name's Joan. I'm Susanna."

☐ At breakfast one morning eight-year-old Cutie-pie pushed her corn flakes away from her, loudly protesting that she would not eat the stuff. More than that, she screamed, "I won't eat any breakfast unless there's something gooder."

Indulgent mother asked, "Well, what would you like for breakfast?"

"I want a worm," Cutie-pie hollered out. "A big, juicy one!"

Again progressive mother, who did not believe children should be frustrated lest they grow up and become left-handed, a missionary, or a musician, sent father to the garden. A few minutes later he appeared with a fat worm. Cutie-pie went into a tantrum. "I want it cooked." So, rolled in butter, it was cooked to a golden brown and brought back to the table. The little lady sobbed and cried, "I want daddy to eat half of it." After a half minute of hesitation punctuated by Cutie-pie's whining, the father closed his eyes, shuddered, and gulped. Half the worm was gone. Then came a tempest as Cutie-pie howled.

"What do you want now?" asked mother. "Didn't daddy eat half the worm?"

"Yes, but he ate the half I wanted!"

☐ 1st parent: Does spanking have any advantages?
   2nd parent: It makes the child smart.

☐ A stranger asked where the nursery was. The church greeter replied, "Down there is the Inner Spancktum."

☐ 1st college student: Ever get on the wrong track?

2nd student: Sure did, but my dad always provided switching facilities.

☐ "Do you believe in spanking your children?" one parent asked another.

"No," came the reply, "but I do believe in giving them a pat on the back, often enough, hard enough, and low enough."

☐ On a New York to Los Angeles flight a peppy youngster ran up and down the aisle, nearly driving everyone crazy. When he smacked into the stewardess, knocking a cup of coffee to the floor, she exasperatingly exclaimed, "Why don't you go and play outside?"

☐ "Mother, am I a canoe?" asked Joan.

"Most certainly not," mother emphatically replied. "Whatever makes you ask that?"

"You're always saying you like to see people paddle their own canoe. And since you paddle me so much, I thought I was a canoe!"

☐ A new family moved into an ultra-modern home in a new development. An endless stream of modern appliances was delivered. One neighbor asked, "Is everything in that home run by a switch?"

Another neighbor, who had seen some of their children tearing up the backyard, retorted, "Everything but the children!"

DISPOSITION

☐ A postman about to start delivering mail on a new route was looking over notations made by a previous mailman. Of one house it said, "Big dog—doesn't bite." Of another, "Mean dog—bites with warning." Then he came across one on which was written in large letters: "Bad-tempered woman!"

☐ The late Bible teacher, Harry Ironside, driving home with his wife after a long and busy Sunday, said, "Please don't speak sharply to me. Do you realize I have preached six sermons today?"

Mrs. Ironside replied, "And do you realize I have listened to you preach six times today?"

☐ When Bible teacher Ralph Keiper and his wife were on their honeymoon, the bride attempted to press the trousers of her husband's new suit with an iron received as a wedding present. When she applied the hot iron, part of the trousers went up in a puff of smoke, leaving a small but gaping hole.

The groom rushed in from the next room, "Is everything all right?"

Whereupon the bride burst into tears as she tried to relate what had happened. "Honey," he replied, "let's get down on our knees and give thanks that my leg wasn't in those trousers!"

DOCTOR OF DIVINITY

☐ Pastor Twiddle received a letter informing him that he was to be the recipient of an honorary D.D. degree. Excited at first, his enthusiasm soon cooled. He explained, "It's bad enough when they call me Reverend Twiddle, but I just couldn't stand to be called Reverend Twiddle, D.D."

DOCTRINE

☐ The teacher of a catechism class required his class to memorize the Apostles' Creed, and to repeat it clause by clause, with each pupil having his own clause. As the recitation began, the first boy said, "I believe in God the Father Almighty, Maker of heaven and earth." The second boy said, "I believe in Jesus Christ His only Son our Lord." The recitation went on till one boy said, "From thence he shall judge the quick and the dead." Then silence fell, which was broken by the next boy in line blurting out, "Please, sir, the boy who believes in the Holy Ghost is absent today."

☐ Two girls from different churches in the same denomination were comparing their catechism classes. "In ours we've gotten as far as redemption," said one.

"Oh," replied the other, "I'm far beyond redemption."

☐ Teacher: Where did evil originate?
Little boy: In the choir.

☐ A lady went back into the Bank of England to transact some business. A clerk asked if she wanted her bonds redeemed or converted.

She replied, "Say, what is this—the Bank of England or the Church of England?"

☐ A church member was asked, "What do you believe?"
He answered, "I believe what my church believes."
"What does your church believe?"
"My church believes what I believe."
"What do you and your church believe?"
"We both believe the same thing."

DOUBLE-MINDEDNESS

☐ Two boys on a bicycle built for two had a hard time climbing up a hill. When they finally reached the top, both were near exhaustion, especially the front boy who said, "I thought we would never make it!"

"We wouldn't have," replied the other, "if I hadn't kept my foot on the brake to keep us from rolling down the hill."

☐ During the Ciivl War one soldier decided to be friends with both sides by wearing a Confederate jacket and Yankee trousers. But Confederate soldiers hit him in the legs, and Yankee marksmen winged him in the chest.

DRIVING

☐ Said a husband, "My wife and I cooperate wonderfully whenever we're out in the car together. She drives while I steer."

☐ When a policeman stopped a motorist for driving without a taillight, he seemed quite agitated. "It's not as bad as all that," said the officer. "I'm not going to give you a ticket."

Came the reply, "It's not the taillight I'm worried about. What's become of my trailer?"

☐ Weeping tears of outrage, the lady driver insisted she had given a turn signal before her car was struck by the man's.

"Look, lady," said the man, "I saw your arm go up, then down, then straight out, then into circles. Are you trying to tell me that's a signal?"

"Goodness," she replied, "the first three signals were wrong. Didn't you see me erase them?"

EARLY RISING

☐ A young Christian asked George Muller, well known for his answers to prayer, to pray that he would get out of bed earlier in the morning.

Muller answered, "You get one leg out, and I'll ask the Lord to get your other leg out!"

☐ Adam Clarke, writer of a Bible commentary, was an early morning riser. A young preacher wanted to know the eminent theologian's secret. "Do you pray about it?" he asked.

"No," was the reply, "I just get up!"

EASTER

☐ A little boy, sitting in an Easter service midst a congregation dressed in its Easter finery, was asked by his mother, "Do you know what day this is?"

Quick as a flash came his answer, "Decoration Day."

EDUCATION

☐ Billy Graham tells the story of a coach who was most eager for a certain ball player to be accepted by the college, so he arranged for an interview between the athlete and the dean. "If you are able to answer one simple question, you can enter college," said the dean. Then he asked, "How much is six and six?"

The athlete thought for a minute, then answered, "Thirteen."

There was silence. Then the coach broke in, "Aw, dean, let him in. He only missed it by two!"

☐ A little girl learned the multiplication table and thought she had exhausted mathematics. With a twinkle in his eye, her grandpa asked, "What's thirteen times thirteen?"

Turning to him with scorn in her eyes, she said, "Don't be silly, grandpa; there's no such thing!"

☐ Commencement visitor: What's that building over there?

Sophomore: Oh, that's our new greenhouse.

Visitor: Since when did colleges start giving freshmen a dormitory all to themselves?

☐ A middle-aged man commented, "My old teacher never forgets her students. Whenever she drops us a note she always addresses us according to our scholastic grade—like Hundred Percent James, Eighty Percent Robert. I had a letter from her yesterday—it began, 'Dear Zero.' "

☐ 1st father: How would you define a college education?

2nd father: A four-year loaf on father's dough which makes you come out half-baked or full of crust.

☐ "Which books, apart from the Bible, have helped you most?" a young college student was asked.

"My mother's cookbook and my father's checkbook."

☐ Said one man, "There must be a lot of knowledge in that college."

When asked why, he retorted, "Because the freshmen know it all when they come in, and the seniors know nothing when they leave."

☐ A farmer had a son at college. At the end of the first year the son came home to announce he stood second in his class.

"Second," said the father, "why not first? What do you think I'm sending you to college for?"

Next year the young man returned home to announce he had won first place that year.

The father looked at him for a few minutes, then shrugged his shoulders, "Can't be much of a college after all."

☐ "Now I want everyone to write a short description of the funniest thing they ever saw," the teacher announced to her class. After five minutes she saw that one of her students had put down his pen, apparently completing his composition. "You haven't finished already?" she asked.

"Oh, yes," was the answer. "'The funniest thing I ever saw was too funny for words."

ENTHUSIASM

☐ A young lady could be seen each evening jumping up and down in front of a corner mailbox. When a neighbor showed curiosity, the girl explained, "I'm taking a course in cheer-leading by correspondence!"

☐ After playing vigorously after school, an energetic boy sat down to supper. He ate his meat and potatoes and vegetables, then a piece of cake. Then a piece of pie and another piece of cake, till there remained one last piece of cake. He asked for it.

"If you eat one more thing," warned his mother, "you'll . . . you'll burst!"

His reply, "Mother, pass the cake and get out of the way!"

ENVY

☐ A mother of three children was talking about her neighbor who had seven. "She's out of this world. She keeps her house clean. She sews all the kids' clothes. She's a good cook. Her children are so talented and so polite. She is active in church and Brownies. She's attractive and so vivacious. She makes me sick!"

EXAGGERATION

☐ A preacher in the habit of exaggerating his stories said to his wife on their way to church, "If I start exaggerating tonight, please make a sign and I'll stop."

In the sermon he began to tell about a big church he had visited as a boy. "It was six hundred feet long," he explained, "three hundred feet wide, and. . . ."

Just then his wife gave him the sign. So he meekly ended his description, "Of course it was just six inches high."

☐ When a little boy told his mother he had caught a fish a mile long, she rebuked him, "Haven't I told you a million times not to exaggerate?"

☐ After a nuclear war had destroyed most of the world, the three survivors discovered they were all Baptists. So they had a Sunday school drive, setting a goal of four. Five came. They reported six.

EXAMPLE

☐ A little girl was showing the bathroom scales in her home to a playmate. "All I know is—you stand on it and it makes you angry."

☐ A father returning from work one day heard his little boy and girl quarreling violently with each other. It looked like they were going to come to blows. "Children, why are you fighting so?"

The little boy answered with an airy smile, "Why, father, we aren't quarreling; we're just playing mother and father."

EXCUSES

☐ When a patient asked if he could see his dentist that afternoon, the dentist replied, "Sorry, not today. I've got eighteen cavities to fill." Then the dentist grabbed his golf bag and headed for the country club.

☐ A man was charged in court with some violation of the law. He pled, "Your honor, I'm a Christian. I'm a new man, but I have an old nature too. It was not my new man but the old man that did the wrong."

To the self-excusing lawbreaker the judge replied, "Since it was the old man that broke the law we'll sentence him to thirty days in jail. And since the new man was an accomplice in the wrong, we'll give him thirty days also. I therefore sentence you to jail for sixty days."

☐ A man with a prison record was discovered trying the doors of a church with a bunch of keys. His explanation, "I was just looking for a place to pray."

☐ A man said he couldn't come to church because he had clothing illness. Asked more about it, he said, "My tongue has a coat, and my breath comes in short pants."

☐ A little boy came home from school with his report card. After his father looked at it, but before he could say a word, the little fellow asked, "What's to blame for this poor report card? Environment or heredity?"

☐ You've heard the tale of the deacon and nominal church member who went fishing together. As evening approached, the godly deacon suggested that they head the boat in toward shore so as to attend the midweek prayer service.

The member said it was impossible to get home on time.

The deacon was honestly sorry about the whole situation and said so. The nominal church member, who never attended prayer meeting anyway, exclaimed, "I couldn't attend tonight. My wife is sick!" And so he continued to bob up and down in the boat, many miles away from his sick wife.

☐ When an important baseball game was scheduled for the next day, the office boy asked for the day off. "For what reason this time?" snapped the manager. "You've already asked time off for your grandfather's funeral four times."

"Tomorrow," replied the boy, "grandmother's getting married again."

☐ A farmer caught a neighbor lad crouching in the branches of his apple tree. "What are you doing up there?" he asked.

"Er—um," stammered the little boy meekly, "I saw one of your apples fall from this branch, and I'm trying to put it back."

FAITH

☐ One night a little four-year-old was being put to bed by his father, who noticed a piece of rope tied to the lad's bed. "What's the rope for?" the father asked.

"I'm praying for a pony tonight," he said firmly, "and that rope is for the angels to tie the pony to my bed."

☐ A lady walking toward a plane said to the pilot who was standing nearby, "Be careful, please. This is my first flight."

The pilot replied, "Don't feel too bad. This is my first flight, too."

☐ A man in great trouble was nevertheless able to sleep each night. Someone asked him how he could sleep under such stress; and he answered, "I've handed the matter over to the Lord, who never slumbers or sleeps. There's no use both of us staying awake all night."

FAITHFULNESS

☐ A business man on a Chicago to New York train asked the porter to be sure and wake him at 3 A.M. to get off at Buffalo. "I'm a heavy sleeper. No matter what kind of fuss I put up—be sure to get me up, for I have important business there."

Next morning the business man wakened in New York City. When he found the porter he bawled him out for fair. A bystander later asked the porter, "How could you just stand there and take all that abuse from that man?"

Replied the porter, "That wasn't anything. You should have heard the man that I put off in Buffalo."

☐ The governor of Rhode Island was attending a banquet which he was going to have to leave early, after bringing greetings before the main course. The waitress brought a roll, then a patty of butter. Later another roll was brought around. When he asked a waitress for another patty of butter, she said, "No, I am sorry."

He said, "Do you know who I am?"

She said, "No."

He replied, "The governor of Rhode Island."

She asked, "Do you know who I am?"

When he said no, she replied, "I'm the waitress in charge of butter."

☐ A small man said to a large man, "If I were as big as you, I would go into the woods, find me a big bear, and pull him limb from limb."

The big man replied, "There are some little bears in the woods, too. Let's see what you can do."

☐ A motorist tried in vain to find a parking spot. He stuck this note under the windshield wiper, "I've circled the block for fifteen minutes. If I don't park here, I'll miss a very important appointment. 'Forgive us our trespasses.' "

On returning he found this note pinned to a parking ticket. "I've circled the block for fifteen years. If I don't give you a ticket, I could be fired. 'Lead us not into temptation.' "

FAREWELLS

☐ A florist sent a bouquet to a pastor and wife starting in a new church that Sunday. Later in the day the florist paid the pastor a visit. The pastor thanked the florist for the bouquet and then showed him the message on the accompanying card, which read, "Sympathy." The florist was shocked. But the pastor assured him of his appreciation for the flowers.

"But you don't understand," explained the florist, "for what bothers me is that the bouquet meant for you must have gone to a funeral. What will they think when they get a big piece that reads, 'Best wishes in your new location'?"

☐ A lawyer was reading the will of a man who had just died. It said, "I leave all to my wife, providing she marries immediately." The lawyer realized it was usual to leave all to the wife, but wondered why the provision requiring immediate marriage.

The explanation came a little later as he continued reading the will. It said, "I want someone to feel bad that I'm gone."

☐ At a farewell for a pastor leaving for a new church a lady looked very sad. "Don't be sorry," said the pastor, "for the next preacher will probably be a much better preacher than I."

Retorted the lady, "That's what they said when the last preacher left!"

FATHERS

☐ A college student, doing poorly, wishing to break the news indirectly to his dad, wrote his brother, "Failed in exams—prepare dad."

Answer came back, "Dad prepared. Prepare yourself."

☐ Two boys were arguing about the devil. "There's really no devil," said one. "It's just like Santa Claus. It's your father."

☐ Two boys were arguing about their dad's greatness. "Mine's greater than yours," said the first boy. "No, he isn't," insisted the second.

"Ever hear of the Rocky Mountains? My dad built them," said the first.

"That's nothing," the other replied. "Ever hear of the Dead Sea? My dad killed it."

60

☐ A father was posing at Christmastime with his college son. When the photographer suggested that the lad stand with his hand on his father's shoulder, the father replied, "It would look more natural if he could place his hand in my pocket."

☐ A little girl wrote, "Dear Santa Claus: Please bring daddy some of whatever sort of hair tonic you use on your beard 'cause my daddy's head is starting to come up through his hair."

☐ A little boy wrote an essay on "My Pop's Tops" which contained this compliment: "My dad never passed sixth grade; yet he's just as smart as if he was in the seventh."

☐ Two boys were bragging about their dads. One said, "My dad went to Penn State." Retorted the other, "That's nothing. Mine went to the State pen."

☐ A little boy ran in from play one evening to the living room where his father was reading the newspaper. "Dad, where did I come from?"

Mother cleared her throat and excused herself to let father answer this long-feared question. Then father cleared his throat and went through a long, careful explanation of how children are born. When he was finally through, junior commented, "That's OK, Dad; but my pal Joe down the street says he came from Omaha and I just wanted to know where I came from."

☐ Teacher (to father): I'm having trouble with your little boy. He steals erasers every week.

Father: That beats me. I bring home a box of erasers every week from the office.

FAULTS

☐ A business tycoon said, "The trouble with most people is that they won't admit their faults. Everyone ought to admit his shortcomings. I certainly would admit my faults if I had any."

☐ One man, after going into a rage and storming out of a committee meeting because the chairman did not agree to his proposal, insisted on making an open apology to the entire organization at a business meeting.

Here's how he apologized, and in pompous tone: "In a recent committee meeting, the chairman and I disagreed. During the discussion which followed, I became emphatic. Still the chairman did not see it my way and I became more emphatic. Before the meeting was over, I became most emphatic. At that point, I retired from the meeting. I would like to take this opportunity," he concluded, "to apologize to the chairman for becoming most emphatic."

FICKLENESS

☐ A girl gave her boyfriend her picture. On the back was this note: "Dearest Love: I love you more every day and always will. I know you will feel the same way about me. All my love forever and ever. P.S. When we break up I want this picture back."

☐ Awakened at his home by a young man pounding on the door, a justice of the peace in Kansas City was asked to perform a marriage ceremony.

"Have you a license?" the justice replied.

"Yes," the prospective groom said. "But you'll have to change the girl's name."

"Did someone make a mistake in filling it out?"

"No, I got the license a day ago and then the girl I intended to marry backed out. So I got another girl!"

☐ 1st student: Here's a card that says, "To the only girl I've ever really loved."

2nd student: I'm going to buy a dozen.

☐ The young sailor stood nervously before his division officer. "Sir, I'm getting married soon, and there's something I've just got to get off my chest."

The division officer replied, "Now tell me your trouble."

"Well, it's like this, sir. I've just got to get this thing off my chest. I'm marrying a girl named Elsie next week."

"Lots of boys marry girls named Elsie," the officer replied.

"Yes, sir," the sailor blurted, "but this tattoo on my chest says Joan."

☐ A girl said to a friend, "I'm not fickle."

"Prove it," challenged the friend.

"I've used the same girl friend four times as a bridesmaid."

FLOWERS

☐ A young mother had just returned from the hospital. Resting on the living room couch she heard her son answer the door. It was the florist with a large bouquet of flowers. Imagine her surprise when she heard her son say, "Take them back. She ain't dead yet."

☐ The occupant of one of the motel rooms entered the motel manager's office with a bouquet of flowers. With sympathetic tone he said, "These are for the maid that cleans my room."

The manager, pleased, responded, "I'm sure she will be happy at this compliment of her fine work."

"Work!" screamed the occupant, "I thought she had expired."

FREUDIAN SLIP

☐ The pastor had made several visits to invite Mr. X to the church service. After the sixth visit, Mr. X reported to his wife, "Guess who came to see me today—Pester Jones."

☐ A little girl had been warned not to say anything about the new minister's big nose. He was coming for dinner. When the bell rang, she opened the door, "Oh, how do you do, Mr. Nose!"

FUNERALS

☐ Somebody thinking they would have fun with the preacher managed to unload a dying donkey on the preacher's doorstep in the middle of the night. When the parson found it in the morning the donkey was dead. He called the veterinarian, "Doc, there's a dead donkey in front of my house."

In on the prank, the vet answered, "Do you ministers take care of the dead?"

"That's right. We do," came the reply, "but first we get in touch with their relatives."

☐ A man who hadn't lived the best kind of life passed away. At the funeral the preacher gave a very flowery description of the man, telling what a good husband and father he had been. Finally, the wife leaned over to her little boy and whispered, "Go up and see if that's your daddy in that coffin."

☐ An English soldier in a French village saw a wedding procession come out of a church. Asking whose wedding it was, he was informed by a Frenchman, "Je ne sais pas." A few hours later the same soldier saw a coffin going into the same church. Curiosity gained the better of him, so he asked the identity of the individual. "Je ne sais pas," was the answer. "Wowie," exclaimed the soldier, "he didn't last long."

FUTURE

☐ It's the year 2000. The city editor of a large newspaper, an efficient lady, is sitting at her desk when suddenly the door opens. A young lady reporter plunks a story down on her desk. "When did it happen?" asks the editor.

"Twenty minutes ago," the girl replies.

"Too old," the editor snarls, tossing the copy into the wastebasket.

Again the door bursts open, admitting another young female reporter with copy in her hand.

"When did this happen?" the editor asks.

"Ten minutes ago," the reporter answers.

"Too late," coldly remarks the editor.

Suddenly the door again opens. A peppy young reporter breaks in, slamming a story on the editor's desk. Once more the question, "When did this happen?"

The peppy reporter, cautioning with her hand, quietly replied, "If you listen, you'll hear the shot!"

☐ One father used to keep valuable papers in the huge family Bible. Birth announcements he filed under *Genesis,* obituaries under *Lamentations,* bills under *Job,* correspondence under *Romans,* medical data under *Luke,* maps for proposed trips under *Exodus,* and financial matters under *Numbers.* Under *Revelation* he had placed a wide variety which did not fit any category.

Pressed for an explanation, he explained, "That's information too important to toss out; and if I keep it long enough, it will be revealed to me what to do with it."

☐ Some winters ago a small Pennsylvania town had a series of disastrous fires which could not be controlled because the fireplugs were frozen. The city council called a hurried meeting to take measures to prevent the recurrence of such a condition. After minutes of hot debate one man jumped to his feet and shouted, "I move that the fireplugs be tested three days before every fire." In a flash another member seconded the motion and the resolution was passed.

GAMBLING

☐ A neon sign partially blinked out in front of a "We Never Close" gambling place in Las Vegas. For several embarrassing hours it read, "We Never lose."

☐ A civil defense warning read, "In case of an air raid go to the nearest slot machine. It hasn't been hit in years."

☐ A man raffled off a horse at a dollar a ticket. The horse died. When the winner came back to complain that the horse was dead, he gave the winner back his dollar.

☐ A little boy asked how a race horse differed from other horses. Came the answer, "It's the only animal that can take several hundred people for a ride at the same time."

GOSSIP

☐ "I've got something to tell you," whispered the gossip. "But listen carefully, because I can tell this only once. You see I promised not to repeat it."

☐ Known to be the worst gossip in the community, a lady came up to a church altar at the end of a service and said to the pastor, "I'd like to lay my tongue on the altar."

His reply, "I'd like to help you but the altar is only fifteen feet long."

☐ 1st boy: We have roast beef or roast chicken almost every Sunday for dinner.

2nd boy: We have either roast preacher or roast soloist.

☐ A month after arrival in a different church, the new pastor learned that a rumor had circulated about him. In effect it said that he had taken his wife to a concert after prayer meeting, had bawled her out as they sat in the front row, then had marched her down the aisle.

He let the rumor circulate for a few weeks, then decided to spike it. During the announcements on a Sunday morning he said, "The story is not true—for four reasons. First, I wouldn't take my wife to a concert after prayer meeting. Second, I wouldn't argue with her in public. Third, I wouldn't create such a scene by marching her down the aisle while the program was still on. And finally, I'm not married."

☐ A lady went to her minister and said she liked him but for one thing. "I'd like to take a scissors and shorten your tie." He kindly agreed. When she was through he asked the same privilege, adding he would like to shorten something on her.

When she reluctantly agreed, he replied, "Put out your tongue!"

☐ A lady was showing a church friend her neighbor's wash through her back window. "Our neighbor isn't very clean. Look at those streaks on the wash!"

Replied her friend, "Those streaks aren't on your neighbor's wash. They're on your window."

☐ Three preachers began discussing the weaknesses of the flesh. "I must confess," said the first, "that I myself am not perfect. In my younger years I swore like a trooper, and even now at times I use profane language."

Said the second, "My recurring fault is alcohol. Of course, I imbibe very infrequently; but at times I am tempted beyond my powers."

"Well, gentlemen," said the third, "my besetting vice is gossip; and I can hardly wait to get out of here!"

☐ A friend called at a home to speak to Mrs. Antwerp, a fine lady but one whose tongue made life miserable for all in the home. The maid opened the door. "I'm sorry, but Mrs. Antwerp isn't here. She's at adult education school taking a course in 'domestic silence.' "

☐ Question: How many persons does it take to make a good conversation?
Answer: Three. Two of them present, and one far enough away to be out of hearing.

☐ Lady to inquisitive pastor: Can you keep a secret?
Lady (when the eager pastor answered yes): Well, so can I!

☐ "It's my policy never to say anything about anyone unless it's something good." The speaker paused, "And boy, is this good!"

GRACE AT MEALS

☐ A little boy went out to dinner with an uncle he had never met. At the restaurant the boy, who had been taught to ask the blessing before meals, bowed his head and said grace. The uncle looked surprised and began eating.
"Don't you pray at meals, uncle?" asked the nephew.
The uncle said no.
"Oh, I see," said the lad, "You're just like my dog—you start right in!"

☐ One steaming hot day when they had guests for dinner, mother asked her four-year-old girl to ask the blessing. "What should I say?" she asked.
"What you've heard me say, dear," mother answered.
Obediently she bowed her little head and out came, "Oh, Lord, why did I invite these people over here on such a hot day as this?"

☐ A little girl was asked if she ever offered a prayer at mealtime. Her answer, "Oh, no! We don't have to. My mother is a good cook!"

☐ A boy unused to the custom of saying grace before meals was visiting in a home where a father said a long blessing. Back home the boy asked his mother, "Why doesn't daddy read what's on the plate before we eat?"

☐ Little boy: Do you say grace at your house?

Friend: Come to think of it—only when mother's serving leftovers.

☐ A man used to often grumble at the food placed before him at mealtime. Then he would ask the blessing.

One day after his usual combination of complaint and prayer his little girl asked, "Daddy, does God hear us when we pray?"

To teach his daughter a lesson on prayer the father solemnly replied, "Why, of course He hears our prayers."

"And does He hear everything we say?"

"Of course," the father said, hoping to teach an additional lesson.

"Then, which does God believe?"

☐ A Christian farmer spent the day in the city. In a restaurant for his noon meal, he sat near a group of young men. After he bowed his head to give thanks for his food, one of the young men thought he would embarrass the old gentleman. "Hey, farmer, does everybody do that out where you live?"

The old man calmly replied, "No, son, some just grunt and go right at it. They're pigs."

GRADUATION

☐ 1st graduate: How did you manage to get your sheepskin?
2nd graduate: I pulled the wool over my professors' eyes.

☐ Father: I'm giving my son a watch for graduation.
Friend: Is it a surprise?
Father: Sure is. He's expecting a sports car.

☐ Neighbor: Congratulations on your son's graduation. Does it cost much to send a son to college these days?
Father: Sure does. It cost me thousands of dollars and all I got was a quarterback.

☐ A young man who graduated from college and seminary hurried out exclaiming, "World, here I come. I have my A.B. and my B.D."
The world replied, "Sit down while I teach you the rest of the alphabet."

GRANDMOTHERS

☐ Child's definition of grandmother: "That white-haired lady that keeps mommy from hitting me."

☐ Someone said a child is a person who is frequently spoiled because you can't spank the two grandmothers.

HABITS

☐ Two preachers were known for their large appetites. A mutual friend decided to run a contest to see which could consume more food. He took them to a restaurant where each ate to his heart's content. When one had reached the limit, the other then started. The second one devoured two steaks, one turkey, two helpings of mashed potatoes, two dishes of corn, two quarts of ice cream, four cups of coffee, one cake, and two pies. He won the contest.

Accepting congratulations on the way out, the winner replied, "Please don't tell my wife, or else she won't feed me when I get home!"

☐ Judge, settling down in dentist's chair: Please pull the tooth, the whole tooth, and nothing but the tooth.

☐ A teacher on her way to school noticed a lady slumped over the steering wheel of her car as it sat parked by a suburban train station. Commuters were hurrying to catch their early morning express. The teacher felt it her duty to offer help to the lady driver bowed over in evident discomfort. "Anything wrong?" she asked.

The lady, half crying, half laughing, explained. "For fourteen years I have driven my husband to the station to catch his train. This morning I forgot him!"

☐ A preacher had a hobby he was always riding. Every sermon he preached somehow brought in baptism. To cure him the deacons hit on the idea of selecting his text for him and giving it to him while he was in the pulpit. The preacher agreed. The first text they read to him was, "Twenty axes."

He seemed puzzled. "Twenty axes," he repeated. "I don't know what anyone would want with twenty axes unless it would be to go down to the river and cut a hole in the ice so one could have a baptismal service."

☐ A taxi driver had his stand located outside a church. One Sunday morning a stranger asked, "What time does the morning service end?"

"I don't know," replied the taxi driver, "but they always have four big noises. So far this morning they've had only three."

HEARING

☐ A lady used to always say to her pastor, "Didn't you give it to them this morning? You sure preached to them today!" One day the weather was so bad she was the only one who came to service. The preacher preached as usual. When he was through, she came up and said, "If they had been here, they sure would have gotten it today."

☐ A small girl was busy reading a book. Her mother asked, "What are you reading about, my child?"
Came the answer, "I don't know, mummy."
"But you were reading aloud, my child," said mother.
"Yes, mummy; but I wasn't listening."

☐ A high school commencement speaker began his address with everyone listening. But then, everything went wrong. A child began to cry. Then a second child joined in. A small boy ran up and down the aisle, soon chased by another lad. The speaker had the sinking sensation which only a public speaker knows when he realizes he has lost his audience.

The speaker tried every trick of his trade. He spoke louder, told a humorous story, stared at the area of disturbance. But to no avail.

Then he tried his last desperate trick. He found one good listener. An elderly gentleman in the first row was looking up, smiling and nodding his head. Concentrating all his attention on this one listener, the speaker gradually gained attention.

After the meeting the speaker asked the school principal to introduce him to the old gentleman who sat in the front row.

"Well, yes, I'll try to introduce you," said the superintendent, "but it may be difficult. You see, the old fellow is stone deaf."

HEART

☐ A little boy insisted on standing up on the seat while riding in the automobile. His mother kept urging him to sit down. Finally, with a frowning face he obeyed. Noticing that his mother was not too pleased, he said, "Well you told me to sit down, and I did. I'm sitting down on the outside, but inside I'm standing up!"

☐ A Quaker woman walking down the street was accosted by a woman in a fit of anger who proceeded to administer a tongue lashing. But the Quaker woman took it graciously. She did not retaliate, even though blameless.

After the episode, a friend said wonderingly, "I marvel that you responded to her with such real Christian grace."

"Ah," said the Quaker woman, "thee did not see the boiling within!"

HONESTY

☐ Salesman: This pair of shoes will last you for a lifetime. They're a good strong pair.

Customer: Just what I've been looking for. I'll take them.

Salesman: Will one pair be enough?

☐ A woman phoned the grocer, "I sent my little boy to your store for two pounds of plums, and I got only a pound and a half. Your scales must be wrong."

Replied the fruit dealer, "My scales are all right, madam. Have you weighed your little boy?"

☐ A clerk had one chicken left in an ice-packed barrel. When a customer asked for a chicken, the clerk pulled it out and said, "The weight is five pounds."

"I want a bigger one," said the customer.

"Oh, I have another one," said the clerk who put the chicken back in the barrel and then pulled the same chicken out and putting it on the scales pressed down until it said seven pounds.

"That's fine," said the customer. "I'll take both of them."

☐ Out in a western town a case was about to open before a judge noted for his rough-and-ready kind of justice. To the assembled court he announced, "I have in my possession a check from the plaintiff for five thousand dollars, and a check from the defendant for ten thousand dollars. I will return five thousand dollars to the defendant. Then the case will be tried on its merits."

☐ On a pleasure cruise in the Caribbean a young lady fell overboard. Soon another figure plunged into the waters, holding her up till a lifeboat reached them. Back on board he was given a party in honor of his valor.

When passengers called for a few words, he reacted, "There's just one thing I'd like to know. Who pushed me?"

☐ A little girl had just bitten her brother's nose in an argument. Her mother said to her, "It's the devil who made you mad."

"No," said the girl, "the devil does get me mad every now and again, but biting my brother's nose was all my idea."

☐ When an elderly landlady rented some rooms to two boys who left without paying, she lamented, "They seemed such nice boys. They had towels from the YMCA."

☐ A church member whose business was real estate said, "This house has both its good points and its bad points. To show you I'm above board, I'll tell you both. Its bad points are that there is a chemical plant one block north and a slaughterhouse three blocks south."

"Tell me the good points," asked the prospect.

"The good point is that you can aways tell which way the breeze is blowing."

HOSPITALITY

☐ "Mother," asked the little girl at dinner, "isn't this roast beef we're having?"

"Yes, dear. Why do you ask?"

Looking right at the visiting minister, she said, "Daddy is such a big tease. He told me we were going to have old muttonhead for dinner tonight!"

☐ Three preachers enjoyed a chicken dinner on the farm of a parishioner. After the meal the farmer took them around the yard. Seeing a rooster with its head lifted high, one minister remarked, "That fellow's pretty cocky, isn't he?"

The farmer's son who had been following them around exclaimed, "You'd be cocky too if you just had three sons enter the ministry!"

☐ Halfway during the sermon the visiting preacher saw a lady leave her seat near the front and hurry out. It turned out to be his hostess for noon dinner. Serving the main course, she said, "I have an apology to make. Reason I left the service was—you said you didn't like common-taters; and since this was the only kind of taters I had prepared, I had to hurry out to make something different."

☐ A visiting preacher was being entertained in a home before the evening service where he was scheduled to deliver a sermon. The hostess had prepared special refreshments. But the guest refused to partake, explaining that a meal would spoil his delivery. After the service, the hostess who had stayed home asked her son how the service went. His reply, "He might as well have et!"

HUMILITY

☐ A man sent a generous check to charity with this note, "I wish to remain anonymous; so I haven't signed the check."

☐ A man was given a medal by his fellow townsmen for being the humblest man in the community. Next day they withdrew the award because the man wore the medal.

☐ An author wrote a book titled *Humility and How I Attained It*. The printer ran out of "I's" and had to use the number "1." The foreword of the book contained this sentence: "I'd like to get more humble, but I have so little to be humble about."

☐ An enthusiastic seminary senior was scheduled to speak Sunday morning in a little country church. Right on the dot he dashed into the church, rushed up the platform steps, and hurried to the pulpit. He pranced through the first part of the service, then came to the sermon. As he began to preach he lost some of his steam. His rapid-fire sentences gave way to more hesitant speech. Finally, overcome with nervousness he broke down. "I've forgotten my sermon," he admitted, and walked off the platform slowly and dejectedly.

An older and wiser official remarked to him, "If you had gone up on the platform like you come down, you would have come down like you went up!"

☐ George Washington Carver, whose scientific work was related to the peanut, said, "When I was young I said to God, 'God, tell me the mystery of the universe.' But God answered, 'That knowledge is reserved for Me alone.' So I said, 'God, tell me the mystery of the peanut.' Then God said, 'Well, George, that's more your size.' And He told me."

HURRY

☐ On a crowded bus a girl unwrapped the kerchief from her hair as she clung to a strap. A gentleman offered her his seat.

"No, thanks," she said, nodding toward the fan spinning near her head, "you see, I'm drying my hair."

☐ As a jet was about to take off, a lady called to the stewardess, "Please tell the pilot not to fly faster than sound because my friend and I want to talk."

☐ At the ticket desk in the Detroit airport a man asked what time the plane left for Chicago. "Eight o'clock," responded the clerk.

"What time does it arrive?"

"Two minutes before eight," said the clerk, failing to mention that Chicago was an hour slower than Detroit.

The man stepped back from the desk. "Do you wish a ticket?" asked the clerk.

"No, I just want to go out and watch that plane take off!"

☐ As the train was pulling out of the station, a young man tossed his briefcase onto the observation platform and swung himself up over the handrail. He stood puffing but victorious as the train gathered momentum. An older man on the platform watched him with disdain. "You young fellows don't keep yourselves in shape," he scorned. "Why, when I was your age, I could carry a cup of coffee in one hand, and run half a mile to catch the 7:45 by the skin of my teeth, and still be as fresh as a daisy."

"You don't understand," panted the young man. "I missed this train at the last station!"

HUSBANDS

☐ A father had been boasting of how he was not afraid of bears or snakes or darkness or storms. After listening him out his little girl commented, "You're really, truly not afraid of anything, daddy, but just mama."

☐ "Who is the boss in your home?" asked one husband of another.

Came the reply. "I am boss in my home. And my wife has authorized me to say so."

☐ Wife to husband: Can you give me a little money?
  Husband: Yes, how little?

☐ Marriage counselor (to wife): Did you wake up grumpy this morning?
  Wife: No, I just let him sleep.

☐ One Sunday morning when a man had promised his wife he would go to church he was nowhere to be found at home. She phoned the locker room at the local golf club. "Is my husband there?"
  The boy on duty answered, "No, ma'am."
  "How can you say he isn't there before I even tell you who I am?" the wife asked.
  "Don't make no difference, lady. They ain't never nobody's husband here."

HYPOCRISY

☐ A little girl, as it neared her birthday, in praying for a present, yelled as loud as she could. Her little brother remonstrated, "You don't have to yell. God isn't deaf."

☐ The owner of a famous racing stable one day passed a place where a farmer was building a high fence around his pasture. The sportsman, curious, asked the farmer, "Why are you building such a high fence?"
  The farmer replied, "I've got a mule that can jump most any kind of fence. I've got to contain him."
  The sportsman said, "Do you mean you have a mule that can jump that fence?"
  "Sure."
  "Then I'd like to buy him," replied the sportsman.
  When the sale was completed, the new owner placed him among his thoroughbreds. He then sent for a famous veterinary surgeon who

trimmed the mule's ears to resemble those of a horse, let his mane and tail grow, and put shoes on his feet. By springtime, outwardly the animal had been transformed into a fine race horse. The experiment proved successful. Prizes were won for hurdle races in many places.

After winning the last race of the season, just as the judges were beginning to distribute the prizes and were approaching the winning animal to award him the blue ribbon, he suddenly reared back on his haunches and with all stops open, brayed like the mule he was.

☐ A minister in upstate New York used to imbibe strong drink on the side. He had it shipped into his home in crates on which would be marked "Books."

One day the station express office phoned him and said, "Reverend, your books are leaking."

IGNORANCE

☐ The famed physicist Albert Einstein, trying to read a menu in a restaurant, realized he had forgotten his glasses; so he asked the waiter to read him the menu.

The waiter fumbled with the menu, then admitted he couldn't read. "I'm ignorant, too, sir," he confessed.

☐ A young preacher in the midst of a group of ministers and laymen spoke about how grateful he was that he had never come into contact with college, and especially seminary. He admitted he had no education and seemed proud of it.

An older pastor asked, "Do I understand you correctly? Are you saying that you are thankful for your ignorance? If so, you have a great deal to be thankful for."

☐ An older minister said to a new preacher who asked for advice, "Tell them what you know. Don't tell them what you don't know for that will take too long."

IMAGINATION

☐ An Irishman woke up in the middle of the night sputtering, "I'm choking! Quick—open the window!"

His bedfellow jumped out all confused and excited.

The Irishman repeated, "Quick—open the window, I'm choking!"

The other fellow fumbled around in the dark, felt the glass, but moaned, "I can't push it up! I can't budge it!"

"Break it then! I'm choking!" said the gasping Irishman.

The other fellow put his fist through it. After the glass fell in a thousand pieces, the Irishman went off to sleep peacefully. In the morning when they awoke, they found the dresser mirror broken.

☐ An absent-minded man, coming in out of the cold, began to warm his hands over an office radiator. After a couple of minutes, a friend remarked, "There's no heat in that radiator. The furnace hasn't been fixed yet."

"Why did you tell me," replied the man. "Just when I was getting nice and warm."

☐ Just before the sermon in a crowded church the preacher said, "I have noticed several Sunday evenings here that the atmosphere has been rather close and stuffy." Then he took from his desk a bottle, and said, "I have a fluid here that will purify the atmosphere and make it comfortable, and I am going to sprinkle it around." He took the cork from the bottle, put some of the liquid in his hands, and sprinkled it around.

Then he said, "After a little while you will feel the effect. You will find the atmosphere freshened when it reaches you, and I should like you to lift your hand when you feel it." Presently people lifted their hands in different quarters.

By and by he said, "It should be reaching the gallery by this time. Will someone in the back of the gallery raise his hand when he feels it?" Presently hands went up in various parts of the gallery, intimating that they were becoming more comfortable.

Then the preacher said, "I am glad you are all so comfortable. It was just a bottle of water, that's all."

INFIDELS

☐ An infidel sneered, "So many things in the world are made wrong. Look at that little acorn on that big oak, and that big pumpkin on that little vine! People talk about an all-wise God at the head of this universe. Now if I had been doing it, I would have put that acorn on the vine, and the pumpkin on the oak."

Just then an acorn fell and hit him on the head.

A listener was heard to remark, "What if it had been a pumpkin!"

☐ When Bishop Phillips Brooks, author of "O Little Town of Bethlehem," was recovering from illness and not seeing any visitors, Robert G. Ingersoll, the anti-Christian propagandist, called to see him. He was admitted by the bishop at once. "I appreciate this very much," said Ingersoll, "especially when you aren't permitting your close friends in to see you."

"Oh," replied the bishop, "I'm confident of seeing my friends in the next world, but this may be my last chance of seeing you."

☐ An infidel, working in a lumber camp in the north woods, said: "If there is a God, I defy Him to strike me dead."

Some time later, his clothing got caught in a machine. While being whirled violently, he shouted the two words, "My God," six times.

A friend stopped the machine, delivered him to safety, and said, "I thought you didn't believe there was a God, and now you have six of them."

☐ At the end of a tour around a large church, an unbeliever said to the godly pastor, "If God doesn't exist, and I believe he doesn't, then you will have wasted your whole life giving it to the service of the church."

The pastor smiled, "If I am wrong, I will have wasted at most fifty or seventy years. If you are wrong, you will waste a whole eternity."

☐ An outdoor gospel service was in progress. A listener began to heckle the preacher, "Christianity hasn't done much good. It's been in the world for nineteen hundred years and look at the state of the world!"

Without batting an eyelash, back came the retort from the preacher, "And soap has been in the world longer than that and look at the dirt on your face!"

☐ An Episcopal clergyman took a seat in a dining car on a train traveling along the Hudson River. Opposite him was an atheist who, seeing the clerical collar, started a discussion. "I see you are a clergyman."

"Yes," came the reply, "I am a minister of the gospel."

"I suppose you believe the Bible."

The clergyman, orthodox in his views, responded, "I certainly do believe the Bible to be the Word of God."

"But aren't there things in the Bible you can't explain?"

With humility the minister answered, "Yes, there are places in the Bible too hard for me to understand."

With an air of triumph as though he had cornered the preacher he asked, "Well, what do you do then?"

Unruffled, the clergyman went on eating his dinner—which happened to be Hudson shad, a tasty fish but noted for its bony structure. Looking up, he said, "Sir, I do just the same as when eating this shad. When I come to the bones, I put them to the side of the plate and go on enjoying my lunch. I leave the bones for some fool to choke on."

☐ An unbeliever was arguing over the story of Jonah and the fish. The believer said, "I'll ask Jonah all about it when I get to heaven."

Asked the unbeliever, "What if he's not there?"

The believer retorted, "In that case you ask him."

☐ The philosopher David Hume wrote an essay on the sufficiency of the light of nature for man's spiritual needs. A noted minister, F. W. Robertson, published a sermon upholding the opposite thesis, pointing out that the light of nature needs to be supplemented by the light of a revelation from God. The two were brought together by mutual friends to debate the matter. When the evening ended, Hume rose to leave. Robertson took a light to show him the way. Hume protested, "Don't worry about me. I always find the light of nature sufficient." But opening the door, he stumbled over something on the steps and tumbled into the street. Robertson jumped down beside him, and holding up his light over the prostrate philosopher to see that he was not hurt, softly but firmly said, "You need a little light from above."

INGRATITUDE

☐ In Vermont a farmer was sitting on the porch with his wife. He was beginning to realize how much she meant to him. It was about time—for they had lived together forty-two years, and she had been such a help, a very willing worker. One day as they sat together, he said, "Wife, you've been such a wonderful woman that there are times I can hardly keep from telling you."

☐ Susan wasn't too inclined to say her prayers one night. "Surely, said her mother, "you ought to say your prayers joyfully, and give thanks for all the good things you have. Think of all the children without nice homes, or clothes, or food, or parents to take care of them!"

"I do think of them," replied Susan, "and it seems to me that they're the ones who ought to say their prayers!"

☐ A man asked an old friend for a loan without interest. The old friend jolted the man by saying he didn't feel the present state of their friendship justified the request.

The man exclaimed, "How can you say such a thing to me? We grew up together. I helped you with your school work. I saved you from drowning. I gave you your start in business. I persuaded my neighbor to marry your brother!"

"Oh, I remember all that. What disturbs me is—what have you done for me recently?"

☐ A man sat in front of an office building selling shoelaces. One executive gave the unfortunate a dime every morning, but never took the laces. One day, the peddler, on receiving the dime, tapped the departing benefactor on the back. "I don't like to complain, sir; but the laces are now fifteen cents."

INTRODUCTIONS

☐ A guest Baptist preacher was being introduced to a large Presbyterian gathering. Said the chairman, "Our guest speaker had trouble with his speech when he was young. A speech therapist told him to put five marbles in his mouth in the morning and speak all day with the five marbles in. Then next day he was to put four marbles in, and speak all day that way. Then next day, three. Next day, two. Then, one. 'Then,' he said, 'when you have lost all your marbles, you will become a Baptist preacher.' "

When the preacher rose, he commented, "That was a marbelous introduction!"

☐ At a banquet in honor of Thomas Edison the toastmaster listed his many inventions, dwelling at length on the talking machine. When the aged inventor rose to his feet, he smiled gently, "I thank the gentleman for his kind remarks, but I must insist upon a correction. God invented the talking machine. I only invented the first one that can be shut off!"

☐ When a speaker at a denomination's annual conference was introduced as a businessman who had made twenty-five thousand dollars in potatoes in Maine, he replied, "That is only approximately correct. It was not in Maine; it was in Texas. It was not in potatoes; it was in oil. It was not twenty-five thousand dollars; it was two hundred and fifty thousand dollars. I didn't make it; I lost it. And it wasn't me; it was my brother!"

☐ A speaker failed to show up for a special service in a small country church. After a hard but unsuccessful search for a substitute, it was learned that a bishop was in town for a holiday. Told of the situation, he consented to speak. In introducing him, the church warden in charge of the service said, "We certainly appreciate the bishop's willingness to help out. We feel bad about bothering such an important man, but we did try to find a poorer speaker, but couldn't."

☐ During his Scotland crusade, Billy Graham had occasion to attend a formal dinner in a castle. He rented some dress clothes. Everywhere were men in top hats and striped trousers. Graham turned to a perfectly attired man at the banquet, "Your grace, I don't believe we've met."

The man replied, "I'm your waiter, sir."

☐ A certain minister was noted for his ability to take a good offering. To the amusement of his parishioners, a lady in the congregation who had trouble pronouncing the word *reverend* introduced him to a friend as "Revenue" Smith.

☐ "The life of a lecturer must be trying," said the chairman to the man she was to introduce in a few minutes. "What do you find most difficult?"

"I think," said the speaker, "that my most difficult problem is to wake my audience up following the remarks of introduction."

☐ R. V. Edman, late president of Wheaton College, was introduced to a lady at a Bible conference. Months later, in another service, she approached with the sixty-four-thousand-dollar question, "Do you remember me?"

Dr. Edman, who met thousands of people annually, had a remarkable ability to recall names. "Yes," came the reply. "You are Mrs. White. I met you at the conference."

"No," she corrected, "my name is Snow!"

☐ The governor of the Virgin Islands was a guest in Washington. The master of ceremonies said the usual nice things, then ended his introduction, "It's a real pleasure to present the virgin of Governor's Island."

☐ A chairman apologized to a visiting preacher that the opening part of the service had taken so long.

The speaker began by saying, "I feel like an Egyptian mummy— pressed for time."

☐ Church member, greeting at door: My name is Smith.

Visitor: Mine is not.

☐ A famous radio preacher was being introduced by a fellow pastor who had been awed by a backstage visit to a large radio station where he had seen complicated electrical equipment, generators, and various "powers of the air." Waxing with increasing eloquence, he ended his introduction thus: "I'm delighted to present the king of electrons, the ruler of the airways, in fact, the prince of the power of the air!"

The startled radio preacher shuffled toward the sacred desk. Finding his voice, he gasped, "I've been introduced to many audiences in various and strange ways; but never have I been presented as his majesty the devil!"

☐ At the opening session of the theological society's annual meeting a substitute chairman stood to bring a welcome from the host school. Informing his audience that he was taking someone else's place, he told the story of President Calvin Coolidge who was awakened by a phone call in the middle of the night. A voice said, "I'm Henry Smith and I'm calling to tell you that John Jones has died."

The president replied, "What's that to me? Why do you call me in the middle of the night?"

Came the answer, "John Jones is postmaster in Burlington, Vermont."

Said the president, "I still don't see what that has to do with me."

The voice replied, "I'd like to take his place."

The president responded, "It's perfectly all right with me, if it's all right with the undertaker."

☐ Public speaker: I'm glad to see such a dense crowd here tonight.

Voice from audience: We ain't so dense as we look!

☐ Ralph Abernathy, a speaker at the Minneapolis Congress on Evangelism, was late in arriving. Because of threats on his life, tight security prevailed. When Dr. Abernathy rose to speak, he apologized for his lateness, commenting, "I'd rather be Dr. Abernathy late than the late Dr. Abernathy."

☐ A seminary student was introduced by a nervous deacon as the speaker in the absence of the pastor. "He is from the Presbyterian cemetery."

The seminarian began, "That was a grave introduction."

☐ Church bulletin: "We are happy to welcome Rev. Gylliam Jansors a sour speaker this morning."

JOURNALISM

☐ A pastor submitted an article for possible publication. A week later the article was returned with this note, "Someone wrote on this paper."

☐ A pastor submitted an article to a magazine for consideration for publication. When he received no reply in a month he wrote again, saying, "As I have other irons in the fire, I would appreciate an answer soon."

By return mail his manuscript was sent back with this scribbled across the top, "Put with other irons."

JOY

☐ Little Janet was visiting her grandfather's farm. Grandpa, a very religious man, always serious and somber, would tolerate no merriment. Seeking relief from the depressive gloom, little Janet wandered out to the barn where she spotted a donkey. Noting its sad look, she said dolefully as she patted its long face, "Poor donkey, you've got grandpa's religion too!"

☐ A businessman wanted to perform some service. At his pastor's suggestion he stood outside the rescue mission on Skid Row inviting the down-and-outers inside. Stopping one unfortunate, the businessman in a most doleful tone invited him in. The down-and-outer took one look at his mournful face and answered, "No thanks. I have enough troubles of my own!"

☐ A Christian called the attention of his guest to a lovely view over fields and stream to a distant snow-capped mountain. The guest rebuked him with the remark, "What pleasure has a heavenly man in an earthly view?"

Later at dinner the guest asked for a second helping of the de-

licious peaches and cream. The host graciously served another helping, then asked his guest, "What pleasure does a heavenly man have
in peaches?"

☐ A junk man came down the street where a woman was sweeping
her walk.

"Any old beer bottles?"

Self-righteously the woman retorted, "Do I look like the kind of
person who would drink beer?"

"Pardon me," apologized the junk man. "Any old vinegar bottles?"

☐ Willie, vacationing with his grandparents, wasn't behaving very
nicely. Grandma had to punish him; so she made him stay in the
kitchen. He whimpered and cried, but Grandma pretended she didn't
notice. After a while she said, "Willie, would you like some Coca-
Cola?"

"No," he scolded. "You're trying to make me happy and you
can't."

JUMPING AT CONCLUSIONS

☐ A well-to-do lady had just registered in a hotel and was being
taken to her room by the bellhop. As they reached a door, she stag-
gered backwards, complaining, "This is terrible. Why—this room is
too small for anybody. I won't go in. Why—it doesn't even have a
bed!"

The bellboy calmly answered, "Aw, come on, ma'am, jump in.
This ain't your room. This is the elevator!"

☐ A deacon was scrutinizing passengers as they alighted from the
train to try to pick out the visiting preacher whom he was scheduled
to entertain but whom he had never seen. Selecting a likely fellow
he asked, "Pardon me, but are you a minister?"

"No," came the curt reply, "it's my indigestion that makes me
look like this!"

☐ A clergyman in Great Britain was doing visitation on his motorcycle. Like most of his fellow ministers, he wore his collar buttoned in the back. The afternoon was raw and sleety. Making a turn he skidded on the slippery street into a telephone pole. The accident was evidently serious. The first to arrive on the scene was a simple-headed boy who tried to help. But when the police arrived the preacher was dead. They asked the boy how the victim was when he had found him. "Well," he said, "when I arrived he was still alive but in bad shape. He had hit the pole so hard it had knocked his head all the way around so that the back of his collar was in front. By the time I got his head around he was dead."

☐ A lady invited several friends to a mushroom steak dinner. When the maid opened the can of mushrooms, she discovered a slight scum on the top. Since her guests were expected momentarily, the lady suggested, "Give the dog a little and if he eats it, it's probably all right." The dog licked it and begged for more, so the dinner was completed.

After the main course, the maid came in to serve the dessert. But her face was ashen white. She whispered in her mistress's ear, "Ma'am, the dog's dead."

There was only one thing to do. Sometime later the guests were reclining in chairs and couches, after the doctor had left, in various stages of recovery after the use of the stomach pump. When the maid came back in, the mistress asked, "Where's the poor dog now?"

Came the answer, "Out on the street, ma'am, where he fell after the car hit him."

☐ Some years ago when someone knocked late one night on his dormitory door, a student at Moody Bible Institute called out, "Who's there?"

A voice came, "It's me. It's Dr. Gray." (Dr. Gray was then president.)

Replied the student, "If you were Dr. Gray, you wouldn't say, 'It's me.' You'd say, 'It's I.' "

The student opened the door and there stood Dr. Gray.

☐ A woman was waiting patiently in a long line for a particular but scarce kind of stocking. Another lady who had been looking at sweaters came down the line and called to a friend, "They've nothing but red ones."

The customer in line for the hosiery exclaimed, "Who wants red stockings."

In fifteen seconds the long line had broken up.

☐ Gifts to Prairie Bible Institute from a certain area began to decline. It was at a time when the school's president, Dr. Maxwell, had undergone two operations for cataracts on the eyes. When a representative of the school was in that area, he tried to find out why giving to Prairie Bible Institute had declined.

He was told, "We heard that Dr. Maxwell is riding around in two Cadillacs!"

Somehow rumor had changed *cataracts* into *Cadillacs*.

☐ An opinionated young man stood in front of a taxidermist store. In the window was an owl which had attracted many sightseers. Anxious to display his knowledge, he said with pompous air, "If I couldn't stuff an owl better than that, I would quit the business. The head isn't right. The pose of the body isn't right. The feet are not placed right."

Before he could finish his evaluation, the owl turned his head and winked at him.

☐ A general met two soldiers near camp carrying a large soup kettle from the kitchen. "Here," he ordered, "let me taste that."

"But, General—"

"Don't give me any buts," roared the general. "Give me a spoon."

"Yes, sir," replied the soldier as he ran to the kitchen for the spoon.

The general took one taste and quickly spat it out. "You don't call that stuff soup, do you?"

"No, sir," answered the soldier, "that's what I was trying to tell you. It's dishwater."

☐ The captain of a whaling ship once wrote in his log, "Mate got drunk today."

The mate sobered up and read the entry, and, knowing the owner of the boat would fire him when they made port, begged the captain to strike it out, promising never to touch another drop. But the captain refused, saying, "Anything once written in that log stays there."

A few days later the mate was keeping the log. At the bottom of the page he wrote in large letters, "Captain was sober today."

☐ A man mentioned to his landlord about the tenants in the apartment over his. "Many a night they stamp on the floor and shout till midnight."

When the landlord asked if it bothered him, he replied, "Not really, for I usually stay up and practice my trumpet till about that time most every night anyway."

☐ A man called up a doctor in the middle of the night, "Doctor, come quick. My wife is very sick. I think she has appendicitis."

The doctor replied, "Your wife couldn't have appendicitis. I took out her appendix myself nine or ten years ago. Have you ever heard of a woman having a second appendix?"

The fellow replied, "No, Doc; but didn't you ever hear of a man having a second wife?"

☐ Six-year-old Steve had picked up some bad words which caused his mother some anguish. On his way out to a playmate's birthday party, he heard his mother's parting warning, "Stephen, I've asked them to send you straight home the minute you use a bad word."

Fifteen minutes later Steve walked in the door. His furious mother ordered him to bed. His attempts to explain were ignored. Later his mother mellowed. Going upstairs she asked, "Tell me, honestly, Steve, just why you were sent home. What did you say?"

Little Steve, humiliated but still angry, exploded, "I didn't do nuttin.' That party ain't till tomorrow!"

☐ A new young salesman, who had just gotten into the living room of a prospective customer, poured a bag of dirt all over the housewife's clean carpet. "Now, I'll show you how efficiently this vacuum cleaner works."

"You'll have to use something else," replied the housewife, somewhat peeved, "because we haven't paid our electric bill for two months."

LARGE FAMILIES

☐ A young couple sent a friend a playpen on the arrival of their sixth child. Her thank-you letter took them by surprise. "The pen is just what we needed," she wrote. "I sit in it every afternoon and read, and the kids can't get near me!"

☐ The parents of a large family reached the entrance to the zoo. A sign read, "Admission 50c per family." Herding his fourteen children through the gate, the father handed the ticket collector one fifty-cent piece. "Are all these your children?" he asked in open-mouthed amazement.

"Every single one of them."

"Well, here's your fifty cents back," said the ticket collector. "It's worth more for these animals to see your family than for your family to see these animals!"

☐ A newlywed was filling out his first income-tax form. In the space marked, "Exemptions claimed for children," he penned in, "Watch this space!"

☐ The late Mrs. P. W. Philpott, whose husband once pastored Moody Church in Chicago, was taking nine of her children on a streetcar. The conductor asked her if they were all her children and if this was a picnic. She retorted, "These are all my children, and it's no picnic!"

☐ A mother with one child called at a home where there were seven youngsters. Seeing their smooth-running household, she asked the parents if they had any domestic help. "Surely with all these children and all the washing, ironing, dishes, and cleaning, you must have some outside help."

At this point the father proudly answered, "No, we don't need any. You see—we raise our own!"

☐ A disc jockey in Memphis received a phone request, "Do you have 'Ten Toes in Tennessee?'"

"No," replied the disc jockey (who didn't recognize this as the title of a record), "but I have a wife and thirteen children in Texas!"

"Is that a record?" the voice on the phone asked.

"No, but it's above average!"

☐ "You know that big family with eight children down the road," said a neighbor. "I bought them a dachshund as a gift."

"Why a dachshund?" asked the other neighbor.

"So they can all pet him at once."

☐ In the Midwest lived a large family of children, from a toddler to a big brother over six feet. This big family never ceased to be a cause of wonder to a little girl across the road. One day some paratroopers, whom the family had never seen, began to practice jumping over their farms. The little girl ran to her mother. "Look, mother, the stork's bringing them full-grown now!"

LOST

☐ Though the preacher announced several times that little Mary Moore was lost and should go to the back of the church, Mary remained on the front seat. When finally reunited with her mother after the service, she told her mother why she hadn't come to the back.

"Why, mother, I wasn't lost. I knew where I was all the time."

□ On a recent overseas flight, a jetliner ran into some very rough weather. It was extremely foggy and turbulent. The pilot made the following announcement over the plane's intercom: "Ladies and gentlemen, I have two announcements to make. One is good news and the other is bad news. First, I'll give you the bad news. We're lost! Now I'll give you the good news. We're making very good time."

□ A little girl found by the rangers in Yosemite Park assured her distressed mother that she hadn't been lost. Then she added, "But I saw a big black bear that was!"

□ A dazed Indian when offered help to find his way out of the forest replied, "Me not lost. Wigwam lost."

□ A hunter wandering dazed in the woods suddenly spied another hunter. "Boy, am I glad to see you. I've been lost a whole day in these woods."

"That's nothing," came the reply. "I've been lost here a whole week."

LUKEWARMNESS

□ When a church caught fire one night, the fire chief hurried to the fire. The pastor was there, and he couldn't resist saying to the chief, "This is the first time I've seen you in church."

The chief replied, "This is the first time I've seen your church on fire."

□ A church member remarked to a visitor, "Our people are a most united church."

The visitor replied, "Praise the Lord for that."

"Just a minute before you praise any more till you hear the kind of unity we have. Our members are frozen together!"

☐ A little boy, building a church with his tiny blocks, asked his father to be quiet.

The father asked why he should be quiet near a church.

The youngster replied, "All the people in church are asleep."

☐ One day in a church service a man was blessed by a spiritual truth the preacher had just uttered, and shouted, "Hallelujah!" One of the deacons slipped over to him and said, "What's the matter with you?"

The fellow replied, "I've got religion."

The deacon answered, "You didn't get it here."

LYING

☐ An insurance agent called at a certain home. A little girl came to the door, saying, "Mother says to tell you that she is not at home."

The insurance salesman smiled understandingly and replied, "Oh, well, just tell her that I said that I didn't call."

☐ A girl made several visits to a soldier recovering from wounds in a veterans' hospital. To get permission for the visit, since only relatives were allowed to see him, she passed herself off as his sister. One day as she came for a visit she walked up boldly to an elderly lady who she thought must be the new lady in charge of that ward. "May I see Lieutenant Barker, please?"

The lady inquired, "May I ask who you are?"

The girl replied, "Certainly. I am his sister."

"Well, well," said the elderly lady, "I'm glad to know you. I'm his mother."

☐ A man coming home from a fishing trip without any fish stopped off at a fish market and said, "I want ten fish but throw them to me so I can tell my friends I caught them."

☐ Mother: Do you know what happens to little girls who tell lies?

Little Debbie: Yes, they grow up and tell their little girls they'll get curly hair if they eat their spinach.

☐ The teacher asked his class to compose a sentence with the word *amphibious* in it.

One boy wrote, "Most fish stories am fibious."

MARRIAGE

☐ 1st little girl (after wedding ceremony): How many wives did the minister say that man could have?

2nd girl: Why, one, of course.

1st little girl: I was sure I heard him say sixteen: four better, four worse, four richer, and four poorer!

☐ A lady filling in a job application hesitated at the question asking for her marital status, then wrote, "Unremarried."

☐ A wife was asked if her husband had lived up to any of his promises he made before marriage.

"Yes, one."

"Which one was that?"

"He said he wasn't good enough for me."

☐ Once when posing for a portrait, the artist asked William Jennings Bryan, "Why do you wear your hair over your ears?"

Bryan answered, "There's a romance connected with that. When I began courting Mrs. Bryan she objected to the way my ears stood out. So to please her, I let my hair grow to cover them."

"But that was many years ago," said the artist. "Why don't you have your hair cut now?"

"Because," twinkled Bryan, "the romance is still going on."

☐ A teen-age girl was examining her grandmother's wedding ring.

"Wow," said the girl, "what heavy and cumbersome rings those were fifty years ago!"

"True," said the grandmother, "but don't forget that in my day they were made to last a lifetime!"

☐ A husband who was experiencing marital troubles was asked, "Were you married by the justice of the peace?"

"Yes," came the doleful reply, "but they should have called him the secretary of war."

☐ Because of a shortage of maids, the minister's wife advertised for a man servant. The next morning a nicely dressed young man came to the front door.

"Can you start the breakfast by seven o'clock?" asked the minister.

"I guess so," answered the man.

"Can you polish all the silver, wash all the dishes, do the laundry, take care of the lawn, wash windows, iron clothes, and keep the house neat and tidy?"

"Say, preacher," said the young fellow rather meekly, "I came here to see about getting married. But if it's going to be as much work as all that, you can count me out right now."

☐ A woman was helping her husband pick out a new suit. The two were in violent disagreement over which one he should buy. Finally she gave in. "Well, I guess you're the one who will wear the suit."

Meekly he answered, "Well, dear, I did figure that at least I would probably be wearing the coat and vest."

☐ When hubby, a church deacon, arrived home from work, his wife had bad news. "The maid quit. She said you spoke insultingly to her on the phone."

"Good night," exclaimed the husband, "I thought I was talking to you!"

☐ A soldier in the front lines was having domestic difficulties. His wife would send him annoying letters. Unable to stand it any longer, he wrote her, "Stop arguing with me. I want to fight this war in peace!"

☐ "My dear wife, I have taken you safely over all the rough spots of life."
"My dear husband, I don't believe you've missed any one of them."

☐ A friend of the couple just married remarked, "It's an ideal match. He loves him, and she loves her."

☐ A suburbanite, sitting at his window one evening, casually called to his wife: "There goes that woman Charley Jones is in love with."
His wife dropped a plate she was drying, burst through the door, knocked over a lamp, and craned her neck to look out the window. "Where, where?" she panted.
"There," the husband said. "That woman in the blue suit on the corner."
"You idiot!" the lady hissed. "That's his wife!"
"Yes, of course it is," he agreed.

☐ Jeanie was playing with her new housekeeping set when one of her little friends dropped in. "Are you washing dishes?" the friend asked.
"Yes," answered Jeanie, "and I'm also drying them, too, because I'm not married yet."

☐ A scientist, contemplating marriage, attacked the problem logically, making two columns, "Marry," and "Not Marry" and listing the pros and cons. Under pros he wrote: children, home, charms of female chitchat; and under cons he penned: terrible loss of time, cannot read in the evenings, if many children, forced to earn one's bread.
He summed up, "Never mind, boy, there is many a happy slave."

☐ "How can I keep my fiancé from spending so much money on me?" asked a thrifty young lady of her mother after he had taken her out for an expensive dinner.

"That's easy," replied the mother. "Marry him."

☐ A man and wife had their first quarrel during the fiftieth year of their wedded life. The man tucked a gracious note under his wife's pillow, "My darling bride, let's put off quarreling until after the honeymoon is over. Your devoted husband."

☐ On their fiftieth wedding anniversary Mr. and Mrs. Henry Ford attended a celebration in their honor. A newsman asked the auto magnate, "To what do you attribute your successful marriage?"

Came the answer, "The formula is the same as used to make a successful car. Stick to one model."

☐ A new bride whispered to her husband as they pulled up to a hotel on their honeymoon, "Let's act as if we've been married a few years."

"It's all right with me, honey," the groom agreed, "but how in the world can you carry four suitcases?"

☐ A Sunday school teacher was showing pictures to her class, asking them to quote some Bible verse which the picture suggested. First picture showed two children with arms around each other. A child raised his hand and offered the verse, "Love one another."

"Very good," said the teacher.

Another picture showed a little girl listening attentively to her mother. Another child correctly offered the verse, "Obey your parents."

Then a third picture was held up. This one portrayed two boys pulling on the opposite ends of the same cat. The children were nonplussed till one little child piped up, "What God hath joined together, let not man put asunder."

☐ An American movie actress was applying for a passport. "Unmarried?" asked the clerk.

"Occasionally," the actress replied.

☐ The old legend tells how the gods took the roundness of the moon, the trembling of grass, the radiance of the light, and by mixing with other ingredients made woman. A week later man complaining that she talked incessantly, begged the gods to take her back.

A week later man came asking to have her back, moaning that without her life was lonely. Three days later man appeared again, begging the gods to please take her back.

This time they refused, insisting he must keep her. Then he said, "I can't live with her and I can't live without her!"

☐ A snake handler married a funeral director. Their towels are embroidered. "Hiss" and "Hearse."

☐ Judge: What's the charge against this man?

Detective: Bigotry, your honor. He's got three wives.

Judge: You dunce. That's not bigotry. That's trigonometry.

☐ Spotting an old friend he hadn't seen since attending his wedding, a fellow exclaimed, "Wowie, do you look good! Where did you get that tan? Been down in Florida?"

"No," came the explanation. "When we were married, my wife and I agreed that whenever she got mad, I would go outdoors till she calmed down."

☐ A lady concerned that she had no husband went to her pastor. He replied, "The Lord has a plan. One man for one woman. You cannot improve on the Lord's plan."

She replied, "I don't want to improve on it. I just want to get in on it."

MEMORY

☐ Invited to give a devotional talk on Daniel at the couples' club, a young churchman had trouble remembering the names of Daniel's three friends who were thrown into the fiery furnace: Shadrach, Meschach, and Abednego. So he decided to write them on the inside of his suit jacket.

Sure enough—as it came time in his devotional to name Daniel's three friends, his mind went blank. Looking inside his jacket, he blurted out: Hart, Schaffner, and Marx.

☐ The master of ceremonies at a denominational dinner got a little confused, even though following the printed order of program which listed prayer by the Rev. John Crow. He announced, "Brother Pray, will you please crow for us."

☐ Embarrassed because he couldn't remember a fellow club member's name, a man tried an old trick. "Do you spell your name with an *a* or an *e*?"

Came the answer, "With an *a*—my name is Small."

MIDDLE AGE

☐ An adult Sunday school teacher asked, "What is middle age?" He received these answers:

"Someone ten years older than yourself."

"When you worry both about how your children will turn out and when they'll turn in."

"When you go all out and end up all in."

MISSIONARIES

☐ A heathen woman was shown a mirror by a missionary. She had never seen one before. She was a painted, ugly woman. Looking into the mirror, she couldn't figure out who that ugly person was. Finally it dawned on her that it was her own image. Then she urgently offered to buy the mirror; but the missionary needed it to shave, so he refused.

But she was persistent. Because of her influential position in the tribe, the missionary sold it to her for a small sum. No sooner had she bought it than she took it, dashed it to pieces on the ground, stamped on it, and exclaimed, "There, you'll never make me look like that again!"

☐ A missionary gave an impassioned plea for young people to consider service on the mission field when they grew up. After the service a small boy asked to see him.

"I think I can guess why you wish to see me. You want to be a missionary when you grow up, don't you?"

"Oh, no, sir," answered the boy. "I just wondered if you had any foreign stamps you could give me."

☐ A missionary came across a tribe of cannibals deep in the jungles. They had just finished a favorite repast. Meeting the chief, he started a conversation. To his amazement, the chief finally confided that he had attended college in the United States. "Do you mean to tell me that you went to college in America and that you still eat human beings?"

"Yes," responded the chief, "but I use a knife and fork now."

☐ A missionary on furlough from hot Africa was doing deputation work in frigid Maine. His host, showing him to his room, pointed out the electric blanket, and explained how to work the controls, since the missionary had never seen one.

During the night the missionary got cold, so he turned the control higher. Toward morning, he warmed up, so turned the control down. After breakfast, when he was about to leave, he thought he should unplug the blanket. When he leaned over to do so, he discovered that the blanket had never been plugged in.

☐ A missionary family serving under the African Inland Mission in the Belgian Congo had just finished their meal. Then came time for family devotions. One of the boys wanted to know what the Bible meant when it spoke of Christians being the salt of the earth. The explanation satisfied him at the time, but when he was being tucked into bed, he asked, "If we are the salt, who is the pepper?"

☐ Opening a barrel just arrived from the homeland, a missionary found several pairs of shoes and rubbers with holes in the bottom. He made this comment to a fellow worker, "The donors did not put their whole 'soul' into their giving!"

☐ A missionary was caught by cannibals. A big, boiling pot began to steam not far away. "Going to eat me?" asked the missionary. "Why don't you taste me to see if you'll like me?" Whereupon he sliced a piece from the calf of his leg and gave it to the chief, who took one bite, said, "Ugh," and almost choked.

The missionary worked on that island for thirty years. He had a cork leg.

☐ A missionary was suddenly surrounded by hostile-looking tribesmen in a South American jungle. Noting their poised spears and poisoned arrows, he knew he had to think of something quickly.

At that moment a plane flew overhead. "See that bird up there," said the missionary. "That's my friend. If you hurt me, that bird hurt you!"

The chief took one glance at the sky, then answered, "That's no bird. That's a Boeing 747!"

☐ Overheard outside a Dairy Queen, a mother's voice to her daughter, "Joanie, here's a shiny new coin. Why don't you take it to church Sunday and give it to missions."

Joanie replied, "Let me tell you what I think would be much better. I'll buy a chocolate sundae and let the cashier give it to missions."

☐ A missionary and his family noticed that a baby elephant's tusks seemed to get in the way of its trunk. Next time they saw the elephant, its owner had tied its tusks back so as not to interfere with its trunk. Soon after that, on furlough, when the missionary family was being entertained in a home, the hostess asked the missionary's eight-year-old son if he had seen anything unusual in Africa.

His reply, "I saw a baby elephant with braces on its teeth!"

☐ A professor of anatomy at a mission medical school in China some years ago, because of friendship with the local war lord, was able to have him send over for dissection by his students the bodies of executed criminals which were constantly available. But too often the bodies were too mutilated to be of use. So the professor of anatomy wrote a polite letter to the war lord asking if, in the interests of science, he could ask his executioners to exercise more restraint.

Came this reply, "Your most honorable communication has been received. In the future I will send the condemned men to you, and you can just kill them any way that suits you best."

☐ Sunday school teacher: Boys and girls, what is the first message a missionary should teach cannibals?

Pupil: To be vegetarians.

☐ Two missionaries were seized by cannibals, bound, and imprisoned in separate huts. In the morning one asked the chief, "Where's my friend?"

Came the answer, "Friend disappeared into the interior."

☐ A missionary on an extensive preaching tour in a remote area had plenty of trouble with his tent which was burning hot in the day, and more than once flooded by a severe storm at night. Asked to describe his problems in one word, he replied, "Intense."

☐ A missionary was telling the wonderful feeling of seeing the Statue of Liberty again after an absence of several years overseas. "I can still hear the guide tell how the little finger on the statue is just eleven inches long."

"Why only eleven inches?" asked his little boy.

After a moment's thought, the father shot back, "Because if it were an inch longer, it would be a foot."

MONEY

☐ "You're an insignificant little runt," said the half-dollar to the dime.

"I may be," said the dime, "but I go to church oftener than you do!"

☐ A citizen, well known for his stinginess, became seriously ill. To everyone's amazement he promised to give one hundred dollars to his local church if he recovered. He made a good comeback to full health, but never made any move to keep his promise. So, the pastor visited him to remind him. "You made a promise to give one hundred dollars to the church if you recovered."

"I made a promise like that?" the skinflint exclaimed in mock surprise. "That shows how sick I really must have been."

☐ A prosperous but stingy businessman was asked for a contribution to a charitable organization. "Yes," he said piously, "I'll give you my mite."

"Do you mean the widow's mite?" asked the collector.

"Of course."

"Well, I will be satisfied with half that much," said the solicitor. "How much are you worth approximately?"

"Oh, about seventy thousand dollars," said the well-to-do businessman.

"Then give me your check for thirty-five thousand. That will be half as much as the widow gave, for she gave all that she had!"

☐ An older Brazilian Christian said to a new Christian, "Romel, if you had one hundred sheep, would you give fifty of them for the Lord's work?"

"Yes, I would."

"Would you do the same if you had one hundred cows?"

"Yes, I would."

"How about if you had one hundred horses? Would you do the same?"

"Sure I would."

"If you had two pigs, would you give one of them to the Lord?"

"No, I wouldn't; and you have no right to ask me, for you know I have two pigs!"

☐ Someone asked, "What is the most sensitive nerve in the human body?"

The preacher answered, "The one that leads to the pocketbook."

☐ The pastor urged his congregation, "Let us give generously—according to what you reported on your income tax."

☐ "I'm going to prove you can take your money with you," said an old miser. Calling together three friends he said, "Here's an envelope with ten thousand dollars in it for each one of you. When I am buried I want you to throw your envelope in the grave with me just before they cover me with dirt."

At the funeral each threw his envelope in the grave. But on the way back their consciences made them confess. Said the first, "I needed some money, so I kept out one thousand dollars, and threw in only nine thousand."

"I kept out half of my envelope," said the second. "I threw in only five thousand dollars."

"I am surprised and shocked at what you did, gentlemen," commented the third. "How could you hold out like that? I threw in my personal check for the full amount."

☐ Fired up by an enthusiastic congregation, a preacher exclaimed, "Brethren, the church ought to stop walking and get up and run."

"Amen," was the rousing response.

Encouraged, he continued, "Brethren, the church ought to rise and and fly."

"Amen," chorused the hearers.

"But, brethren," the preacher paused so they would get the full effect, "it will take money to make the church run; it will take finances to make the church fly."

Frigid silence followed. Then someone muttered, "Let the church walk."

☐ The greatest surprise of Mary's life was receiving half a silver dollar for her fourth birthday. She carried the coin about the house, and was seen sitting on the stairs admiring it.

"What are you going to do with your silver dollar?" her mother asked.

"Take it to Sunday school," said Mary promptly.

"To show your teacher?"

Mary shook her head. "No," she said, "I'm going to give it to God. He'll be as surprised as I am to get something besides pennies."

☐ 1st member: What was your worst predicament ever?

2nd member: Being caught in church at offering time with only a twenty-dollar bill.

MONUMENTS

☐ The proud possessor of a diamond was asked where he got it.

He replied, "Yes, it cost fifteen hundred dollars. My father gave it to me. It was like this: My father died and in his will he said, 'Here is fifteen hundred dollars for my son, with which he is to erect a stone to my memory!'"

And pointing to the diamond, he said, "That's the stone!"

☐ Walking through a churchyard when he was a small child, Charles Lamb amused himself by reading the inscriptions on the tombstones. His eyes grew wide with surprise at the glowing praise offered to departed ones. At length, he turned to his older sister, "Where are all the naughty people buried?"

☐ "I admire Dr. X so much," said the wife. "He is so persevering in the face of difficulties. He reminds me of patience sitting on a monument."

"Yes," replied her husband, "but what I'm concerned about is the number of monuments sitting on his patients."

MORALS

☐ A teacher absent three days from school had her place taken by a substitute who, after telling a story, usually ended by saying, "This is the moral, boys and girls."

When the regular teacher came back, they told her they liked her better than the substitute because, they said, "You have no morals."

☐ A man visiting a penitentiary in Atlanta, Georgia, saw clerks doing beautiful handwriting. The warden commented, "That's their trouble; they're in here for forgery."

MOTHERS

☐ Six-year-old Margy hated to bring her friends home after school. When they marched through the kitchen, Margy's mother scolded them for dirtying her clean floor. If they took something to eat, they were warned about crumbs.

One day Margy's friend volunteered, "My mother doesn't care how much I mess things up at home."

After a moment of silence, Margy sighed longingly, "I wish I had a nice dirty mother like you've got!"

☐ A little girl, asked what she wished to be when she grew up, answered, "A mother."

When asked if she wanted boys or girls, she replied, "I don't want any children. I just want to be a mother."

☐ A five-year-old boy said, "Mommy, when I grow up I'm going to get you an electric iron, an electric stove, an electric toaster, and an electric chair."

☐ When a mother reprimanded her two sons because they were having a fight with water pistols, they reassured her, "Don't worry mom. We won't get water on anything. We're using ink."

☐ A bride of several months was sawing away at the end of a ham. "Why," asked a neighbor, "are you sawing off the end of that ham?"

"Because my mother always did it," the bride replied.

A few days later the neighbor met the bride's mother. "Your daughter tells me you always saw off the end of a ham before you bake it, and I wonder why."

"Frankly," the mother replied, "I do it because my mother did it. Why not ask her?"

The neighbor phoned the grandmother who lived in the same town. The grandmother let her in on her secret. "I have never owned a baking pan large enough to hold a ham. Why do you ask?"

☐ A little girl asked her daddy to tell her a story. He related a tale involving slaves. "What's a slave, daddy?" she asked. He explained as best he could. When he was through, she looked at her daddy and asked, "Is that what mommy is?"

☐ A little girl, shown pictures of her mother and father on their wedding day asked her father, "Daddy, is that the day you got mother to come to work for you?"

☐ After dinner one Mother's Day a mother was washing the dishes when her teen-age daughter wandered into the kitchen. Horrified to see her mother at the sink, she exclaimed, "Oh, mother you shouldn't have to do dishes on Mother's Day."

The mother was touched by this seeming thoughtfulness and was about to take off her apron and give it to her daughter, when the daughter added, "You should wait till after midnight!"

MOTIVATION

☐ The fond parents stood by Donna's bed as she said her evening prayer. "Dear Lord, please send the lovely snow to keep the sweet little flowers warm all winter." As she jumped into bed, her parents glowed with pride.

As her mother and father were about to leave the room she smiled mischievously, "I sure fooled Him that time. I really want the snow so I can play with my new sled."

☐ American athlete: How come you turn out such fast runners?

Russian athlete: Perhaps it's because our coaches use real bullets in their starting guns.

☐ A toad fell into a rut in the road and could not seem to get out. When he called to a passing toad for assistance, the other toad replied, "If I help you, I may fall into the rut with you. Then there would be two of us who are trapped." So he hopped on. Later, to his surprise, he saw the trapped toad hopping down the road. "I thought you couldn't get out of that rut."

Came the reply, "I couldn't—but a big truck came along and I had to!"

NAMES

☐ At the end of a first and very difficult appointment with a new patient, the psychiatrist asked, "I send my bills out every two weeks. Where should they be sent?"

"Doctor," replied the patient, "don't worry about me. You will get every cent I'll ever owe you or my name isn't Alexander the Great!"

☐ Officer: Did you know you were speeding? What's your name?

Motorist (seeing policeman get out book): Ambrose Aloysius Xcyjichasmochysian.

Officer (putting away notebook): Don't let me catch you speeding again.

☐ Eating dinner at a monastery, a man was served his favorite—fish and chips. On a tour of the kitchen later, he met a gentleman he thought might be the cook; so he asked him if he was the cook.

"No," came the answer, "I am Friar Fish."

Spotting a second man in the kitchen, he put the same question to him, and got this answer, "I'm Chip Monk."

☐ A seminary grad in his first church was teaching the men's class. He remarked how much Webster's Dictionary meant to him. "I don't know what I would do without Daniel Webster's dictionary. I certainly owe a lot to that man—Daniel Webster."

One of the men, realizing the young pastor had gotten his historical characters mixed up, called out, "Not Daniel. You mean *Noah,* don't you?"

The pastor turned to the speaker, and in firmest of tones replied, "Noah built the ark."

☐ On one of his trips a college president was introduced to a lady by the name of Mrs. Large. "That name will be easy to remember," he thought. When they parted a few minutes later, he said, "It certainly was a pleasure to meet you, Mrs. Stout!"

NEWSPAPERS

☐ When a clergyman declined an invitation to a public hearing because of pressure of duties, the papers printed this explanation, "The pastor was unable to be present because he is very occupied with the cuties of his congregation."

☐ An article described the coming Sunday morning service, "The pastor will preach and there will be special sinning by the congregation."

☐ A news story: "The pastor will preach his farewell address. The choir will sing, 'Break Forth into Joy.'"

☐ This item: "The guest preacher will speak on 'How to Keep Your Sanity in the First Presbyterian Church under the direction of Pastor John Jones.'"

☐ This item: "The New England superintendent surprised the local congregation of his denomination last Sunday morning. The superintendent preached a good sermon."

☐ An angry man stomped into the office of a newspaper, waving the latest issue of the paper. In the editor's office, he nearly exploded, "What's this? You've announced my death, and I've never been more alive than I am right now. It's a downright disgrace. What are you going to do about it?"

"I'm so sorry," replied the editor. "We'll make the matter right. I'll put your name in the birth column tomorrow!"

☐ The small town newspaper carried this report, "The eastern superintendent of the Methodist denomination will speak at the Sunday morning service, after which the church will have to be closed for needed repairs."

☐ A factory advertised in the local paper for a night watchman. That night the factory was robbed.

OMISSION

☐ A little boy prayed one night, "Forgive me for all the naughty things I did today, and for all those I planned, but didn't get done."

☐ "Please, sir," said Don nervously as he came into the classroom, "should I be punished for something I haven't done?"

"Of course not," said the teacher kindly.

"Please, sir," said the boy with a sigh of relief, "I haven't done my homework."

ORCHESTRA

☐ Relating the events of the church service, a boy told his father that one horn player's toupee fell off and into his instrument. "What happened after that?" asked the father.

"Oh, the horn player spent the rest of the evening blowing his top."

☐ Violinist in church orchestra: My son has loosened one of the strings in my violin and he won't tell me which one.

☐ When a Salvation Army band was scheduled to give its annual concert in a local church, the newspapers had this caption: "Regular annual bad concert Wednesday evening."

☐ A newly organized church was giving its first concert. At the end of the first number, while the leader was making a few introductory remarks, the trumpet player leaned over to ask the trombonist, "What number do we do next?"

"The Battle Hymn of the Republic," the trombonist answered.

"Oh," gasped the trumpeter, "that's what I just finished playing."

☐ Orchestra leader to new church member: Do you have any musical ability?

New member: All I know how to do is take a full rest between the sheets.

PARENTHOOD

☐ Hearing Junior cry, mother asked, "What's the matter, dear?"

He whimpered, "Daddy hit his thumb with a hammer."

"You shouldn't cry over that; you should laugh," said mother.

"That's the trouble," replied Junior, "I did laugh."

☐ One morning a boy asked his father how wars started. "Well," said dad, "suppose America quarreled with England and—"

"But," interrupted the mother, "America would never quarrel with England."

"I know," said the father, "but I am only taking a hypothetical instance."

"You are misleading the child," protested the mother.

"No, I am not," shouted the father.

"Never mind, dad," put in the boy; "I think I know how wars start."

☐ A policeman found a man sitting on the front steps of a house at two o'clock in the morning. "What are you doing here?" he asked.

"I've lost my key," replied the man, "and I'm waiting for my children to come home and let me in."

☐ At a meal one evening a little child said, "Father."

The father retorted, "Don't speak, shh."

A few moments later the little child said, "Father."

The father replied, "Shh, don't speak."

At the end of the meal the father said, "You can speak now."

It was dessert time then. Replied the boy, "Oh, it's too late, father. There was a caterpillar on your salad and you ate it."

☐ Before he was married, an expert on child psychology said, "I have four good ideas on how to raise children but have no children."

Some years later he confided, "I have four children and no ideas."

☐ Writing an essay on "parents," a child at school included this sentence: "We get our parents when they are so old that it's rather hard to change their ways."

☐ "Ten Commandments for Parents" was the title used for his lecture by a young student of child behavior.

After marriage and the arrival of his first child, the title was modified to "Ten Hints for Parents."

After the second and third were born, the topic became "Some Suggestions for Parents."

After the fourth child, he quit lecturing.

☐ Mother and dad were trying to teach their little girl the value of money. So they asked her to keep a written account of how she spent her allowance. One day as she was about to buy something she said, "Mother, since you and dad made me write down everything I spend, I really stop and think a while before I buy anything."

Mother and father were beaming—till their little girl added, "I never buy anything that I can't spell."

PASTORS

☐ A minister spotted a woman coming up the front walk. Looking more closely he saw it was his leading troublemaker, Mrs. Queen. Hiding in his study, he let his wife handle the caller. An hour later he opened his study door and hearing nothing, called down to his wife, "Has that terrible gossip gone?"

There was a moment of painful silence, then the minister's wife called up, "Yes, dear, she went sometime ago; but Mrs. Queen is here now!"

☐ A pastor had received a call from another church to become its minister. The pastor's twelve-year-old son was talking with a neighbor. "Dad's upstairs praying about it, but mother's downstairs packing."

☐ A pastor and his wife were getting into a heated discussion over the relative merits of their respective families. "Well, I do admit— all my relatives are better than yours, but you do have a better mother-in-law than I."

☐ A little boy swallowed a dime. His frantic parents sent for the doctor. But his kid sister asked, "Why didn't you send for the preacher?"

"Why the preacher?" asked the parents.

"Because he can get money out of anything."

☐ A preacher stood at the door after service shaking hands and unthinkingly repeating after every parishioner's remark, "That's good!"

A lady approached, "My husband's in the hospital in intensive care. The doctor's doesn't give him much hope."

The pastor nodded sweetly, "That's good!"

☐ The assistant pastor, making the announcements, wondered why people laughed when he said, "The pastor will be gone tonight, and we will be having a service of singing and praise."

☐ Two neighbors were talking of a new pastor who had been in town for half a year. Said one, "I hear he suffers from foot and mouth disease: he won't visit and he can't preach."

PASTORS' WIVES

☐ Alone, back home in the parsonage after speaking at a banquet, a minister asked his wife, "Which one of my after-dinner talks do you like the best?"

His wife replied: "I only heard you give it once—it went like this—'Darling, I want to help with the dishes tonight.' "

☐ Pastor's wife to head trustee: "Well, if you can't give my husband a raise, how about the same pay more often!"

☐ A pastor was told by his doctor that his wife should have had her tonsils removed when she was a little girl. He had the operation performed, then sent the bill to his father-in-law.

☐ Policeman: Why didn't you report the robbery at once? Didn't you suspect anything when you came home and found the drawers opened and their contents scattered all over?

Pastor's wife: No, I just thought that my husband had been looking for a clean handkerchief.

☐ When a minister was dressing before making some pastoral calls he couldn't find his cuff links. He fumed, fussed, and fretted around the house, then stormed in a rage. His wife was in tears by the time he left. His first call was on an old lady who, because of a stroke, was confined to her bed. Yet she was most cheerful. Next he called on a middle-aged man who had just been informed his condition was incurable. Yet the parishioner showed no resentment. His final visit was to a semi-shut-in, a poor old lady whose only room was an attic. Yet she was sweetly looking forward to her heavenly home.

Back home he exclaimed to his wife, "Honey, how wonderful is God's grace. Nothing is too hard for it!"

"It is marvelous," replied his wife, "but there is one thing it doesn't seem to have the power to do."

"What's that?" puzzled the preacher.

"It doesn't seem to have the power to control the minister's temper when his cuff links are misplaced!"

PATIENCE

☐ An American businessman was trying to hurry the normal embarkation process at the Rome international airport. Shoving ahead of others at the customs desk, he explained curtly, "I have to make the ten o'clock plane for New York."

At the immigration desk he fussed, and at the currency control window he fumed.

Finally, when he was restlessly waiting his turn at the immunization section, a man standing behind him tapped him on the shoulder. "Don't be overanxious sir," he said. "These things all take time, but the plane won't leave before we do."

"What makes you so sure?" snapped the businessman.

The stranger smiled politely. "I'm the pilot."

PHARISEES

☐ A minister asked a man, "Why don't you go to church?"

Quick as a flash he answered, "The dying thief didn't join a church and he went to heaven."

"Have you been baptized?" the questions continued.

"The dying thief never was," came the answer.

"Do you give to missions?"

"No, the dying thief never did."

"Well," said the minister, "the only difference between you and that fellow is that he was a dying thief and you are a living one."

☐ On a Saturday night a man stole a horse. On Monday morning the police found him very near where he had stolen the horse two nights before. The police asked, "How come you did not get far away from here yesterday? You had all day Sunday to get away."

The man replied, "Oh, I want you to know that I have strong scruples against traveling on Sunday."

☐ A lady said to the preacher at the door, "Everything you said in your sermon was wonderful and fitted someone or other I know."

PRACTICING WHAT YOU PREACH

☐ A third-grade teacher asked her class, "Why did the Puritans come to America?"

A little boy answered, "To worship in their own way and make other people do the same."

☐ During a fourth-grade class lesson a little boy passed this note to the little girl across the aisle: "Dear Peggy, I like you. Do you like me? John."

The teacher intercepted the girl's penciled answer. "Dear John. I do *not* like you. Love, Peggy."

☐ "The new handyman has stolen three of our towels; he's a thief!" exclaimed the husband.

"Which towels?" the wife asked.

"You remember," he replied, "the three we got from the motel at Disneyland."

☐ A Sunday school teacher was much exasperated at the inattention of her class.

"Will you shut up while I teach you about the love of God!" she shouted.

☐ Termites had eaten through a large stock of pamphlets in the mailing room of the University of California at Berkeley. Maintenance men who made the discovery said the pamphlets were entitled, "Control of Termites."

PRAYER

☐ "Hey!" shouted the passing motorist. "Your house is on fire!"
"I know it, stranger," nodded the mountaineer.
"Then why aren't you doing something about it?"
"I am. I'm praying for rain."

☐ A little boy, playing on the roof, began to slip toward the edge. Immediately he began to pray, "Oh, Lord, save me! Save me!" Then, "Never mind, Lord, I'm caught on a nail!"

☐ "Do your folks have prayer before breakfast?" one little boy asked a playmate.

"No," replied the playmate, "we have prayers before we go to bed. We're not afraid in the daytime."

☐ A young salesman went to his minister with a problem. "I would like to get married but I don't make quite enough to support a wife. And my girl is getting tired of waiting. What should I do?"

The minister thought for a moment, then said, "Why don't you pray for a raise?"

"Oh, no," exclaimed the young man, "I couldn't do that. You see, my boss doesn't like me to go over his head."

☐ A little girl told a friend that her brother had set traps to catch some poor harmless birds. The friend asked if she had done anything about it.

"Oh, yes," the girl replied, "I prayed that the traps might not catch the birds."

"Anything else?"

"Yes, then I prayed that God would keep the birds from getting into the traps."

"Was that all?"

"Then I went and kicked the traps all to pieces."

☐ When children were evacuated from a war area because of threatened bombing attacks, little Janet was going to bed, her first night in the country. Repeating her usual, "Now I lay me down to sleep," she improvised a postscript. "And God, please protect daddy and mommy from those bombs. And dear God, please take care of Yourself—because if anything happens to You, we're sunk!"

☐ The pastor asked Bobby, "Do you say your prayers every night?"

"Not every night. Some nights I don't want anything!"

☐ A little boy taken on a tour of government buildings in Washington was introduced to the chaplain of the Senate. Later he asked his father, "Does the chaplain pray for the Senate?"

"No," said the father, "he stands up, looks at the Senate, then prays for the country."

☐ A farmer whose barns were full of corn used to pray, "O Lord, supply the needs of the poor; please feed them." Yet when anyone in need asked for corn he would reply that he had none to spare.

One day his little boy, overhearing his father pray for the needy, said, "Daddy, I wish I had your corn."

"What would you do with it?"

"I'd answer your prayer."

☐ When D. L. Moody was holding a series of meetings in a church on the outskirts of London, England, a minister, called on to pray, went on longer than the evangelist wished. So, in a firm but kind voice Moody announced, "While the good pastor is finishing his prayer, we will sing a hymn."

☐ A minister prayed loudly. His voice thundered through the sanctuary. A little boy was asked what he thought of the prayer. He thought a minute, then answered, "If that man lived nearer to God he wouldn't have to pray so loud."

☐ A little girl was overheard by her mother asking God to make Boston the capital of Vermont. "Why do you pray like that?" asked the mother.
   "Because I said so on my geography exam this afternoon!"

☐ A church member who owed money to another member and who was quite slow about paying back the loan prayed in the midweek meeting, "Give us faith—a devil-driving faith." Under his breath the brother to whom he owed the money prayed, "Amen, and give us a debt-paying faith, too!"

☐ Two little brothers knelt for their usual bedtime prayers. Johnny prayed first, finishing this way, "Amen. Good evening, Lord. Now stay tuned for Jimmy."

PRIDE

☐ A mixed-up celebrity confessed, "I used to be terribly conceited, but my psychoanalyst straightened me out, and now I'm one of the nicest guys around."

☐ A young man received a medal from an organization which used extravagant language to praise his accomplishments. Jubilantly the prizewinner went home and proudly repeated the words to his mother. Then he asked, "How many great men are there in the world today?"

His mother replied, "One less than you think."

☐ After a serious operation a lady was still in a coma. Her worried husband stood at the foot of her bed. "Well," said the nurse reassuringly, "at least her age is on her side."

"She's not so young," said the husband, "she's forty-three."

At this point the patient moved slightly, and quietly but firmly murmured, "Forty-two."

PRIORITIES

☐ As they were strolling away from a church nursery, Mrs. X exclaimed to her husband, "George, that isn't our baby. It's the wrong carriage!"

Mr. X countered, "Keep quiet. This one has rubber tires."

☐ A supersalesman sold a complicated filing system to a thriving business. Three months later the salesman paid the company a visit. "How is the filing system working out?"

"Magnificently," replied the president, "out of this world."

"And how is your business doing?" asked the salesman.

The manager smiled. "We had to give up our business in order to run the filing system!"

PROCRASTINATION

☐ A fellow in a basket on a pulley rope which traveled every hour over a deep gorge, remarked to the operator of the pulley, "The rope must be quite strong."

"Oh, yes," came the reply, "it has a ten-year guarantee; and the guarantee doesn't run out till tomorrow."

PROFESSORS

☐ A professor moaned to his wife, "I'm not popular enough with the fellows to rate a nickname."

"Oh, yes, you are," replied the wife. "You do have one. They call you Sanka."

Later that evening the professor's curiosity overcame him and he searched the kitchen till he found a package of Sanka. The label read, "More than 98% of the active portion of the bean has been removed."

☐ A college class asked its professor many hard questions, some not so intelligent. "Any fool can ask more questions than a wise man can answer," the exasperated prof exclaimed.

"Yes," said one of the students. "We found that out on the last exam you gave us."

☐ At the college pool for a swim, a professor was approached by a co-ed who had accidentally dropped her camera in the deep end.

"Why don't you ask one of the young fellows who are much more agile?" asked the prof.

Cutely the co-ed replied, "Prof, I'm in your economics class; and honestly, you can go down deeper, stay down longer, and come up drier than any teacher I know!"

☐ A science professor in a boys' school possessed an uncanny knowledge of life. You could show him the bone of any animal, and he could name the animal. Give him the scale of a fish and he would not only name the fish but tell you where it lived and when it spawned. His was the world of animals. One day the boys tried a trick on the professor. They got the skeleton of a bear, stuffed it with cotton, sewed over it the skin of a lion, fastened on its head the horns of an ox, and on its feet they glued the hooves of a wild buffalo. They made a good job of it.

Then one afternoon, when the professor was taking his after-lunch nap, they opened the door of his study and carefully set up their monstrosity. Behind the door, they let out an unearthly growl.

The professor stirred, then tumbled off his cot and bolted to his feet, alert with fear. Then through their peepholes, the boys witnessed a surprising change. The old professor rubbed his eyes, looked at the fierce teeth, the horn, and finally at the split hooves. He exclaimed, "How wonderful—it's herbivorous, not carnivorous!" And he went back to finish his nap.

☐ A Monday lecture was being delivered in a seminary classroom. Many students were drowsily nodding, worn out from the long trips and preaching assignments of the previous day. One young man fell asleep and advertised the fact in no uncertain drone.

"Wake him up!" said the professor to the student next to the sleeper.

Quick as a flash the student retorted, "You wake him up! You put him to sleep!"

☐ An absent-minded seminary professor was guest for dinner in the home of the seminary dean. "Please pass the nuts, professor."

Replied the prof, "I'm afraid most of them are going to flunk!"

☐ A theological professor began to dream that he was asleep in front of his class. He woke up to find out he was.

RADIO

☐ A church service was being broadcast. When it came time for the pastoral prayer, the minister asked, "Lord, comfort those who are afflicted by the radio today."

☐ A pastor on his regular daily radio program used to read the letters from his listeners and announce the amount of the donation which accompanied each letter. Once after the letter-reading he resumed, "And now, dear funds. . . ."

☐ A radio pastor who had just finished a sermon on Adam and Eve and his family was floored to hear the announcer say at the end, "Will Cain kill Abel? Be sure to tune in at the same time next week to find out."

REAPING

☐ A lady schoolteacher was pulled over to the side of the road by a policeman for failing to stop at a stop sign. She was given a ticket which ordered her to appear in court early the following Monday morning. Soon as court opened, she went at once to the judge and told him she had to be at her classes. She asked for an immediate hearing of her case.

"So," said the judge sternly, "you're a schoolteacher. Now, you sit right down at that table over there, and write 'I went through a stop sign' five hundred times!"

☐ An invading army came across some farmers engaged in spring planting. "Go ahead and sow," scoffed the invading colonel. "Our army will do the reaping."

The farmer replied, "I hope so. I'm sowing hemp."

☐ In China the father of a family decided to take out the grandfather to some lonely spot in the desolate wilderness and leave him to die of hunger, exposure, or wild beasts. After all, the grandfather was useless and a drain on the meager family groceries. The father took along his little boy.

At the end of the two-day trip, the little son said to his father, "Father, I'm glad you brought me along. For now I know where to bring you when you get old and useless."

☐ A judge in Ohio sentenced a nineteen-year-old boy, who had referred to a police officer as a "pig," to spend three hours in a pigsty. The boy admitted he had learned a lesson.

Someone was heard to comment, "I hope none of these kids ever calls a policeman a crocodile."

RECKONING

☐ One day an actress tried to take her tiny white poodle through customs. She knew it was against the law, but because poor little dogs suffer away from their masters, she tried to smuggle him through, covering him up under her coat. Smiling her prettiest, the actress sailed up to the customs barrier. Everything went splendidly—until her coat barked.

☐ On a vacation trip to the Adirondack Mountains a man and wife from Vermont met a quiet, pleasant couple from New York. All four of them had a grand time together. Later, the gentleman from Vermont made up a nice album of snapshots he had taken of the other couple and mailed it to them in New York. The gift was never acknowledged, until one day a big-city lawyer appeared and asked the gentleman if he had prepared the album. "Sure," was his reply. "Did they get it?"

"It was received all right," said the lawyer. "And I'm representing the man's wife in a divorce suit. You see—she wasn't the woman in the album!"

RETORT

☐ When Lady Astor's seat in the British Parliament was being contested by a candidate from the Labor Party, his argument was that hers was a rural constituency and she knew little about farm life. In a face-to-face public debate he shouted, "Why should she represent it? I should like to ask her if she knows how many toes a pig has?"

Quick as a flash Lady Astor replied, "Take off your boots, man, and count them!"

☐ An irate woman approached a guest speaker after a rather strong and pointed sermon. "If you were my husband," she stammered, "I'd —I'd put poison in your coffee."

"And if you were my wife," countered the speaker, "I'd drink it."

☐ On a cold, dark, damp morning a bus driver had already suffered almost continuous insults from the passengers boarding and leaving his overcrowded bus. At one corner a flippant young man swung onto the steps, quipping, "Hi, Noah! Is the ark full?"

"We're pretty packed," drawled the driver, "but I'm sure we can always use one more monkey!"

☐ Back in the days when perfume was considered wrong to wear, one lady on leaving church sniffed the pastor a bit and said, "You have some perfume on."

He sniffed a bit, then said, "You don't have."

☐ A rather forward young fellow let the local minister know he didn't like him. "If I ever have a son who is a fool," he said on meeting the minister on the street, "I'll make a preacher out of him."

"Indeed," responded the preacher, "how come your father didn't send you to seminary?"

☐ "Fifteen dollars is a lot of money for the three minutes you spent pulling my tooth," said the patient to the dentist.

"If you wish," came the calm reply, "I can pull the next one more slowly."

☐ Jones was awakened at 2 A.M. by his new neighbor who complained, "Your dog is barking. I can't sleep."

Before Jones could answer, his neighbor hung up. Furious, Jones could scarcely contain himself till he thought of an idea. Exactly at 2 A.M., next morning, he phoned his neighbor. "I have no dog," he said. Then he hung up.

☐ 1st man: I've been behaving so well these days that I wonder how I'll ever get my coat on over my wings.

2nd man: What you need to worry about is—how will you get your hat on over your horns.

☐ Samuel Johnson boasted that he could spontaneously create a joke on any subject. "Make one on the king," someone suggested immediately, thinking they had him, for no one dared to joke about royalty.

Came Johnson's quick response, "The king is not a subject."

☐ "My talent is to speak my mind," said a hotheaded woman to John Wesley.

"Woman, God wouldn't care a bit if you would bury that talent," replied Mr. Wesley.

☐ Rabbi and priest were seated together at a school dinner. Said the priest, "Rabbi, when are you going to break down and enjoy this delicious ham with me?"

Replied the rabbi, "At your wedding, Father. At your wedding."

☐ Wife: Look at the old clothes I have to wear. Anyone visiting would think I was the cook around here.

Husband: Not if they stayed for dinner.

SACRIFICE

☐ When her small son refused to eat his spinach, a mother said, "Son, we must not waste our food. Think of all the little boys and girls who are starving in Africa and India and many parts of the world."

Without hesitation he pushed the spinach toward her. "Here, mommy," he said, "save it for them."

☐ A hen and a hog, traveling together, passed a church that displayed next Sunday's sermon topic, "How Can We Help the Poor?"

After a moment's meditation the hen suggested, "I know what we can do. Why don't we give them a ham-and-egg breakfast?"

"That's easy for you to say," replied the hog. "For you that's just a contribution, but for me it would demand total commitment."

☐ In a New York store there was an exhibit of all kinds of crosses in a window. Underneath was a sign which read, "Easy Terms."

SANCTIFICATION

☐ A Sunday school teacher thought he would impress his class with the fact that God was the creator of all, and so he asked, "Bobby, tell me, who made you?"

Whereupon the boy looked up and said, "Well, to tell you the truth, I ain't done yet!"

☐ A Bible class teacher emphasized how Jesus intended to make Simon into a stable, solid character, indicating His purpose by calling him Peter (which means "rock") the first time He met him. But the teacher also pointed out how slow the process seemed, as Simon so often vacillated so unsteadily. "But," he summed up, "the Lord did want to 'Peterize' Simon."

"Even though," piped out a member of the class, "the apostle tried to 'Simonize' Peter."

SELF-DENIAL

☐ During the preliminaries of a large meeting of Christian workers in the city of Indianapolis, this announcement was made, "On Thursday evening at 6:30 the Self-Denial Club will hold a turkey dinner with all the trimmings."

☐ A church bulletin board carried this announcement: "Special speaker at noon meetings each Wednesday in Lent will be Dr. P. Q. Misque, the highest paid clergyman in New England."

☐ A mother handed out sheets of colored paper at her little girl's birthday party and told the children to share the only pair of scissors she placed on each of the four tables.

One of the little girls asked, "What does share mean?"

"Share," a friend whispered, "is what you do when you have just one of something and your mother is looking."

☐ In an ultramodern shop featuring twenty-seven varieties of fried-cakes, was a neat, hand-printed sign, "Our Donuts Have Fewer Calories."

Thinking that she might possibly pick up a new culinary trick, a lady asked the waitress an innocent question about the interesting slogan: "Do you have any idea how the cooks are able to make doughnuts less fattening?"

The obliging girl leaned forward and answered in a low voice, "Don't tell anyone—but we serve them a bit smaller here than any-where else."

SERMONS—LONG

☐ The sexton had been laying new carpet on the pulpit platform and had left several tacks scattered on the floor. "See here," said the parson, "what do you suppose would happen if I stepped on a tack right in the middle of my sermon?"

"I guess there'd be one point you wouldn't linger on."

☐ The sermon was running overtime. Suddenly a lady remembered she had forgotten to turn off the roast. She wrote a note to her husband, who without looking at it, but just out of habit because he was an usher, walked up the aisle and handed it to the preacher. This is what he read, "Go home and turn off the gas!"

☐ The sermons were always just twenty minutes in length. One day the preacher went one hour and twenty minutes. When asked why, he explained, "I always put a Life-saver in my mouth and when it melts I know the twenty minutes are up. But in my hurry I put a button in my mouth by mistake!"

☐ A man who hadn't gone to church in his life went to his first service. His friend tried to answer his questions. When the pastor came on the platform, the newcomer asked, "What's this mean?" and his friend told him. When the offering plate was passed, he wanted to know all about it. After he had preached thirty minutes, the minister took his watch out. "What's that mean?" asked the stranger.
Replied the friend, "Doesn't mean a thing!"

☐ A homiletics student asked his professor if a good beginning and a good ending were the making of a good sermon.
The professor replied, "Yes, if they come close enough together!"

☐ A retired bishop was once asked by a newly ordained preacher, "What should I preach about?"
The elderly man thought a moment, then replied, "Preach about God and preach about twenty minutes."

☐ On a blizzardy Sunday morning only two showed up for church, the preacher and one member. "Should we have a service?" the preacher asked.
"I'm just a farmer," the parishioner replied, "but if it was feeding time on my farm and only one animal showed up, I'd feed him."
So the preacher announced a hymn and the congregation joined in. He prayed, read the Bible, made the announcements, took up the offering. Then he preached for a whole hour. After the service the preacher asked the member how he liked it.
Came the answer, "I'm only a farmer, but if at feeding time only one animal showed up, I'd feed him. However, I wouldn't give him the whole bag of feed."

☐ The sermon had gone on for a long, long time. A visitor leaned over to the person next to him and whispered, "How long has he been preaching?"

The reply, "Almost thirty years."

"Oh," said the stranger, "guess I'll stay. He ought to be through soon."

☐ A minister preached a very short sermon. He explained, "The dog got into my notes and chewed them up."

At the close of the service a lady visitor made this request, "If your dog ever has pups, please let my pastor have one of them!"

☐ Wife (to husband as pastor waxes longer and longer): Hope he quits soon. I just remembered I forgot to turn off the electric heater before we left for church.

Husband: Don't worry. It won't burn long. I just remembered that I forgot to turn off the tap in the bathroom.

☐ A preacher spoke twenty minutes on Isaiah; twenty minutes on Ezekiel; twenty mintes on Jeremiah; twenty minutes on Daniel. Then he said, "We now come to the twelve minor prophets. What place will I give Hosea?"

A man reached for his hat, saying, "I'm leaving. Give Hosea my place."

☐ A young preacher was to address a Southern Baptist gathering in Alabama. His wife, who often reminded him to preach short sermons said, "I'm giving you an envelope in which is a message. You are to open the envelope just before you speak." Just as he was being introduced he pulled the envelope from his pocket, ripped it hurriedly open and read this one word: KISS. The preacher seated to his left couldn't help noticing the message and remarked, "What a wonderful wife you must have!"

Then the speaker whispered back, "The word stands for 'Keep It Short, Stupid.' "

☐ Before building a new church, pastor and people agreed that the pastor would have the say regarding the pews, and the people should design the pulpit. Finally, the building was completed and the time came for the first service. As people came in and sat in the last row, the pastor pushed a button. Suddenly the back pew moved right up to the front. When another row was filled, again by pushing a button the motorized pew slid right up behind the first pew.

Came time for the pastor to preach. Pleased with himself at the way he had gotten the folks up front, he began his sermon in the pulpit the congregation had designed. Ten minutes after he started, the pulpit disappeared through the floor.

☐ A young pastor preached long sermons. When people began to stay away, he defended himself, "I've tried to give them the milk of the Word."

"Pastor," said a parishioner, "I prefer to have the milk condensed."

☐ A man preached and preached. First, people began to walk out one by one; then by two's, as husbands and wives departed. Then whole families went out. Finally, only one man remained, staying right to the end. "Pardon me, sir," asked the speaker, "but I noticed you have stayed to the end and would like to ask why."

Came the reply, "Because I'm the next speaker."

☐ A minister enthusiastically exclaimed to his congregation, "Every blade of grass is a sermon!"

During the week, a member passing the parsonage and noticing the minister cutting his lawn called out approvingly, "That's the idea, pastor; cut your sermons short!"

☐ At a Bible conference one of the speakers went far beyond his allotted hour. As he ended, he apologized to the next speaker. "I hope I haven't trespassed on your time."

Someone on the back seat could be heard muttering, "He wasn't trespassing on time; he was infringing on eternity."

□ After a rather long, painful sermon, a visitor was asked to make some comment on the discourse. His observation, "To be immortal one need not be eternal."

□ A preacher stepped into the pulpit one Sunday morning with a Band-aid on the side of his face. He explained at the start of his sermon, "I cut myself while shaving. Guess I was meditating on my sermon."

One high schooler whispered to his pal, "He should have meditated on his shaving and cut his sermon."

□ Orating endlessly on the immortality of the soul, the preacher said, "Mountains, beautiful as you are, you will be destroyed, while my soul will not. Ocean, mighty as you are, you will eventually dry up, but not I."

□ 1st member: He's a long-winded preacher.
2nd member: He may be long—but never winded.

□ 1st preacher: Why do crowds come to hear your sermons, but not mine?
2nd preacher: Because when I say, "in conclusion," I conclude; but when you say "lastly," you last!

□ Preacher: I now come to my final point; well, er-er, at least my semifinal point.

SERMONS—PREPARATION

□ A small daughter watched her father prepare a sermon. "Daddy, does God tell you what to say?"

"Of course, my child," her father answered. "Why do you ask?"

"Then why do you scratch so much of it out?"

☐ As a pastor was about to begin his Sunday sermon on a sultry summer morning, an usher opened two windows near the front for cross ventilation. A sudden gust of wind blew his notes out the window and out of sight.

"Folks," said the pastor, "I did have a message for you. Now I guess I'll have to trust the Lord."

☐ "With your gift of gab," said a young minister to an older, successful clergyman, "I wonder why you spend so much time on your sermon. Many are the times I've written a sermon and caught a fish before breakfast."

"Well," replied the mature preacher, "all I can say is, I'd rather have eaten your fish than listened to your sermon!"

☐ Spurgeon told about a vicar who had heard his bishop deliver a stirring lecture on the need for diligent study. After the lecture the vicar disagreed with the bishop. "Why," said the vicar, "often when I am in the vestry I do not know what I'm going to talk about; but I go into the pulpit and preach and think nothing of it."

The bishop replied, "And you are quite right in thinking nothing of it, for your church officials have told me that they share your opinion!"

☐ In Practice Preaching class in seminary each student had to deliver three sermons with the sermons written out in full. A certain student with a fair amount of cash, and not too distinct a call to the ministry, secured the services of a not-too-ethical nearby college student to write out these sermons for him. Both of them were so well written that the entire theological faculty decided to attend his third sermon. A few days before delivery date, the seminarian heaped some abuse on his student ghost-writer. On the day of his third sermon, the seminarian began to preach, read the first five pages in booming tones; but when he turned to page six, he found only this statement scribbled in large letters: "From now on, you meanie, you're on your own."

☐ Young preacher: You don't mean to tell me you spend hours preparing a sermon. Doesn't the Bible promise that when we speak our mouths will be filled?

Older preacher: Yes, but the filling is back farther and up a little higher.

SERMONS—REACTION

☐ A minister's son was asked, "Does your father ever preach the same sermon twice?"

After a moment's reflection he replied, "Yes, he does; but I think he hollers in different places!"

☐ President Coolidge was once asked after a Sunday morning church service what the preacher's subject had been. He replied, "He preached on sin."

"What did the preacher say about sin?" the questioner continued.

Coolidge answered, "He was against it."

☐ Four-year-old Annie was in church for the first time. The minister, up high in his pulpit, was earnest and vigorous. His voice rolled out over his congregation in tempest tones as he waved his arms and twisted his torso. Completely fascinated, little Annie, clutching her father's arm, asked worriedly, "What do we do if he escapes?"

☐ A minister was presenting the truth that God knows who best grows in the sunshine experiences of life and also who develops best in the shade. He illustrated, "You know that you plant roses in the sun, but if you want the scarlet shrubs known as fuchsias to grow they must be put in a shady corner."

After the service a lady said, "Reverend, you don't know how much your sermon helped me." The preacher beamed. His sense of achievement soared till the woman added, "I never did realize before just why my fuchsias wouldn't grow!"

☐ A husband, unable to attend church on a Sunday morning when the preacher was candidating for the pulpit, asked his wife, "Was he sound?"

Her reply, "He was all sound!"

☐ A preacher who had been invited the third time to a church, had unwittingly preached the same sermon each time. He was presented with a gift as he boarded the train. Opening the package he found a watch without any mechanism inside. Instead there was a note which read, "If you ever preach that same sermon here again we'll give you the works."

☐ A long-winded sermonizer was shaking hands with his congregation at the door. One of them became mixed up a little; and instead of calling him "reverend," said, "neverend."

☐ A small boy asked his twelve-year-old sister, just as the sermon concluded, "Now, is it all done?"

"No," she whispered back, "it's just all said. Now we must go out and do it."

☐ The new minister preached on "sin." At the door afterward, a nice elderly lady commented, "You are marvelous. I never knew what sin was till you came here."

☐ An evangelist who never prepared his sermons but announced he could open his Bible anywhere and preach from that text, opened to this text one night: "This is the third time I am coming to you." He tried to begin, but no words came. He leaned over the pulpit and repeated the text. He repeated the text a second time, leaning over a little more. The third time he leaned too far, and fell into a man's lap. He got up full of apologies and embarrassed.

"Oh, forget it," said the man. "You certainly warned me enough that you were coming."

☐ "Folks," said the preacher, "the subject of my sermon tonight is Liars. How many in the congregation have read the thirty-ninth chapter of Mark?" Nearly every hand went up immediately. "You're just the folks I want to preach to. Mark has only sixteen chapters."

☐ A minister bought butter from a lady member of his congregation. One day he was ten cents short for his pound of butter. "That's all right," said the saleslady. "I'll take it out in preaching."

Rather annoyed, the pastor replied, "But I don't have any ten-cent sermons."

"Oh, that's all right. I'll hear you twice!"

☐ A visiting preacher halfway through his sermon began to talk loudly and wave his arms around. When a baby began to cry, his mother rose to take him out. "Never mind the baby," said the preacher; "he's not bothering me."

"The baby may not be bothering you," the mother retorted, "but you're sure bothering the baby!"

☐ After a rambling sermon a homiletics professor was asked, "How many points should a sermon have?"

His answer, "At least one."

☐ Outside after the service, one member asked another, "Wouldn't you say our guest preacher this morning was somewhat dogmatic?"

The other replied, "I would go more than that—I would say he was bulldogmatic!"

☐ Preacher (in midst of sermon describing his travels to Mount Sinai): I stood there on the edge of the mountain with a great abyss yawning before me.

Listener (to person sitting next to him): I wonder if the abyss was yawning before he arrived on the scene.

☐ "Know why they say he's a great preacher?"

"Why?"

"Because at the close of every sermon there's a great awakening."

☐ A poet received a note from a young boy. "Your new book of poems is funny and I like them. I read them in church. They were a lot better than the sermon. P.S. Please don't tell my daddy about the sermon because he's the pastor."

☐ A preacher always placed his notes on the pulpit in rather a conspicuous manner. After church one Sunday a teen-age lad asked, "Why do you shove your notes out so everyone can see them?"

Came the answer, "I wish to be a noted preacher."

☐ Two old saints were discussing a sermon just delivered by a student in seminary. "I thought it was divine," said the first. "It reminded me of the peace of God. It passed all understanding."

"Funny, I thought it was divine, too," said the other, "only it reminded me of the mercies of God. I thought it would endure forever."

☐ A visitor to a church noticed the preacher had a pitcher of water and a glass on the pulpit. Several times during the sermon the preacher took a sip of water. After the service someone asked the visitor how he liked the preacher.

"Fine," came the reply, "but he's the first windmill I've seen that was run by water."

☐ The guest speaker had been addressing the congregation for some time when suddenly the loudspeaker konked out. Raising his voice, he asked, "Can you hear me in the back row?"

A man called back, "No."

Whereupon a man in the front row stood and shouted out, "I can hear and I'll change places with you."

☐ After a fine sermon a lady gushed complimentarily. "Whenever I have to speak, even to just a small group, I get all jittery and nervous. But when you preach you seem so unconscious."

SERMONS—STEALING

☐ Billy Sunday, it is said, sometimes took other preachers' sermons and preached them. Once after he had preached one of Gypsy Smith's sermons, the Gypsy took him to task. "You preached my sermon almost word for word," he accused Sunday.

"But after you preached it that night when I heard you," said Sunday, "you sang, 'Pass it on'; and that's what I'm doing."

☐ One day G. Campbell Morgan, great Bible expositor, walked into a meeting where Mel Trotter, converted drunkard, was about to preach. Trotter was startled because he was going to preach one of Morgan's sermons. After the service Trotter apologized for using one of his sermons.

Morgan seemed surprised and said, "Don't charge that thing up to me."

SEXTON

☐ A man stood wistfully at the edge of the crowd as it peppered the bride and groom with confetti that cluttered up the church entrance in unsightly fashion. "Are you related to the bride? Are you thinking of the past when she was just a little girl?"

"No," was the reply, "I'm the sexton thinking of tomorrow!"

☐ The sexton of a large church which had meetings of one kind or another scheduled every day had many extra demands shoved on him. Asked how he could maintain an even disposition with all the aggravation, he explained, "I just puts my feelings in neutral and lets them push me around!"

☐ The sexton of a church set the church's clock by the firing of a cannon from a nearby army post. Becoming acquainted with the soldier who fired the cannon for retreat each evening, the sexton asked, "Do you fire this cannon at the same time every night?"

"Yes," replied the soldier. "At six on the dot, and I time it carefully with this watch. I check it every day by the jeweler's clock about a block from here."

Several days later, the sexton entered the jeweler's shop and began talking to him. "That's a mighty fine clock you have there," he said pointing to a timepiece in the window.

"It keeps perfect time," answered the jeweler. "In fact, that clock has not varied a second for two years."

"That's a wonderful record."

"Yes, we have a perfect check on it, too. Every evening at exactly six o'clock, they fire a cannon over at the fort, and this clock is always right on the dot."

☐ A sexton was going through the pews after an evening service, straightening up a little. A lady who had lingered to talk with a friend was about to walk away without her purse. Spotting her handbag in the pew, the sexton said, "Don't forget your purse. For if you leave it, someone might find it and think it was an answer to their prayers."

☐ After he was on the job for a few weeks, people discovered that the new sexton could play the piano very well. Every now and again he substituted for the pianist. Asked how he could do both jobs, he replied, "I watch my keys and pews."

☐ After six months on the job the new sexton was approached by one of the trustees who half-complaining said, "I notice you go out and get your hair cut on church time."

"Yes," replied the sexton, "my hair grows on church time."

"But it all doesn't grow on church time," replied the trustee.

Came the sexton's retort, "I didn't get it all cut."

SLEEPING IN CHURCH

☐ At a Sunday dinner table a lady asked her husband, "Did you notice the mink coat on the lady in front of us in church today?"

"No," admitted the husband, "I was dozing."

"Huh," retorted the wife, "a lot of good the sermon did you!"

☐ "Are you acquainted with John Jones?"

"I should say I am. We've slept in the same church pew for over twenty years!"

☐ A preacher confessed to periodic bouts of insomnia, then added, "But I have a sure-fire remedy. When I wake up in the night and can't get back to sleep, I go over some of my sermons in my mind. And to my delight, I find that my sermons have the same effect on me that they had on some of the members in my congregation."

☐ 1st boy: Churches should be air-conditioned.

2nd boy: Why?

1st boy: It's not healthy for people to sleep in a stuffy room.

☐ Just before the sermon the preacher announced, "If you sleep during the sermon, please do not snore. You might wake up the deacons!"

☐ 1st boy: I found out why people fall asleep in church.

2nd boy: Why?

1st boy: The longer the spoke, the greater the tire.

SUMMER CAMPS

☐ 1st mother: When your little boy goes off to camp, do you feel like you're losing a son?

2nd mother: I look at it this way. I'm not losing a son, I'm gaining two frogs, three turtles, and a garter snake.

SUNDAY

☐ Six-year-old Robert had been taught that Sunday was not a day for play. One Sunday morning his mother found him sailing his toy boat in the big puddle in the backyard. "Bobby," she scolded, "don't you know it's wicked to sail boats on Sunday?"

"Don't get excited, mother," he matter-of-factly replied; "this isn't a pleasure trip. This is a missionary boat going to India."

☐ Dining with a family, the minister asked, "You never go fishing on Sunday do you, Bobby?"

"Oh, no, sir!"

"That's right, Bobby. Now, can you tell me why you don't go fishing on Sunday?"

"Yes, sir," said Bobby. "Pa says he doesn't want to be bothered with me."

☐ A woman was asked if she noticed any change in her husband since he joined the church. "Why, yes, I do," she reported. "Before he joined, when he did any carpenter work on Sundays, he would carry his hammer and saw on his shoulder. Now he carries them under his coat."

☐ The minister was very strict about keeping Sunday. After prayer meeting he spoke to one of the deacons. "I understand you went to the ball game last Sunday instead of coming to church."

"That's not true!" responded the deacon. "And what's more, I still have one of the fish to prove it."

SUNDAY SCHOOL

☐ Ruth came home from her first visit to Sunday school, eating a chocolate bar.

"Where did you get it, Ruth?" asked her father.

"I bought it with the nickel you gave me. The preacher met me at the door and got me in for nothing."

☐ In the course of the Sunday school lesson the teacher tried to illustrate a point by speaking of a vacuum. One little fellow didn't know what vacuum meant. So the teacher asked for a volunteer to explain its meaning. One fellow raised his hand immediately.

"A vacuum is. . . . A vacuum is, is. . . . I know what it is. I can't explain it, but I got it in my head."

☐ A Sunday school teacher was visiting one of her class members. "Which do you like better—public school or Sunday school?"

Without a moment's hesitation the little boy replied, "Sunday school."

The teacher beamed. Then she asked, "Why? Any particular reason?"

"Oh, yes," said the little boy, "because I have to go only once a week!"

☐ Joe had been promoted from the primary to the junior department at Sunday school. He was most happy about his progress. Coming out of Sunday school he met his former teacher, whom he liked a great deal and regretted losing as a teacher. "Mr. Smith," he exclaimed, "I wish you were smart enough to teach me next year!"

☐ A Sunday school teacher was impressing her pupils with the prodigious rate at which light travels. "Just think," she pointed out, "that light comes to us from the sun and stars at the speed of one hundred eighty-six thousand miles a second. Isn't it wonderful?"

"Not so much," said Bill; "it's downhill all the way!"

☐ Members of a Sunday school class after their teacher returned following illness: "Oh, we thought the substitute teacher was OK, but she wasn't as good as you on the piano. She had to use both hands."

☐ "I want you to understand," said the teacher, "that it is the law of gravity that keeps us on this earth."

"Please," asked little Elsie, "how did we stick here before the law was passed?"

☐ A Sunday school teacher was telling his class about the crowns which would be given as rewards to the saints.

"Tell me," he asked his class of boys, "who will get the biggest crown?"

Bobby piped up, "The one that's got the biggest head."

☐ "What's heredity?" asked a Sunday school teacher.

One boy said, "If grandparents have no children, and parents have no children, then it's pretty sure the children won't have any children."

☐ Teacher: Any questions?

Pupil: If angels have wings, how come they had to climb up and down Jacob's ladder?

☐ A little girl went with her Sunday school class to the Natural History Museum. Back home that evening her father asked her how she had enjoyed herself.

"Very much, daddy. Our teacher took us to a dead circus."

☐ It was Jean's first time at Sunday school. Back home her mother asked her if she had given her offering to Jesus.

"No," replied Jean, "but I gave it to the teacher. You see—Jesus wasn't there."

☐ Teacher to unenthusiastic pupil: Why do you come to Sunday school?

Pupil: Because the Sunday school won't come to me!

☐ On a rainy day the teacher said, "My, it's pouring cats and dogs!"

"I know," said Johnny, "on my way I saw several poodles!"

☐ At a Sunday school picnic Mrs. Smith won the ladies' rolling-pin throwing contest. Mr. Smith won the sixty-yard dash.

☐ 1st boy: If I'm good today, my father will give me a quarter.

2nd boy: My father wants me to be good for nothing.

☐ A teacher was telling the story of John the Baptist, of Herod's promise to Salome to give up to half the kingdom, and of how she asked for John the Baptist's head on a plate. "What would you have said," she asked the class, "if you had been Herod?"

One little lad piped up, "I would have told her that John the Baptist's head wasn't in the half of the kingdom I was going to give."

☐ Two small boys seated at the Sunday school party put their grimy little hands side by side on the white tablecloth.

"Mine's dirtier than yours!" shouted one, triumphantly.

"Huh," the other snorted. "You're two years older'n me."

☐ A Sunday school teacher related the story of the rich man and Lazarus, how the rich man died and went to hell, and how the beggar Lazarus died and was carried away into a place of delight. Then the teacher asked the class which they would rather be: Lazarus or the rich man?

One little fellow piped up, "The rich man in this life, and Lazarus in the next."

☐ A Sunday school teacher asked his class, "What shape is the world?"

A little boy expressed more truth than he realized when he answered, "My daddy says 'the worst shape it's ever been.' "

☐ With all the children in Sunday school trying hard to raise money for the new building, the preacher's son, also eager to help, was trying to save all his nickels. He found it hard.

One night he prayed, "Please help me save my money for the building—and don't let the ice cream man come down the street!"

☐ A little lad went home from Sunday school all excited. His mother, who never bothered with spiritual matters, asked him why he was so excited.

He said that his Sunday school teacher had told him that the Bible was God's Word, God's Book.

His mother readily agreed, "Why yes, my boy; the Bible is God's Book."

The little fellow, with puzzled expression, said, "Mom, do you really mean the Bible in the parlor is God's Book?"

"Yes, my boy," replied the mother.

Then the little fellow excitedly exclaimed, "Then don't you think we ought to send it back to God? Because we never read it."

☐ A teacher asked his Sunday school class, "Why did the priest and the Levite pass by on the other side?"

Little Butch, after serious thought, replied, "Because the poor man had already been robbed."

☐ Johnny, somewhat spoiled, was not taken to Sunday school till he was four years old. Because he had been rarely away from his mother's side up to this time, she anxiously asked him on his arrival home, "Did you cry, sweetie?"

"Nope," Johnny piped brightly, "but the teacher did."

☐ Sunday school teacher: Class, never do anything in private that you wouldn't do in public.

One pupil: Hurray! No more baths.

☐ Teacher: I will use my hat to represent the planet Mars. Do you have any questions?

Pupil: Is Mars inhabited?

☐ Little Raymond came home from Sunday school swollen with importance. He explained his enthusiasm to mother. "The superintendent said something nice about me in his opening prayer this morning."

"And what did he say?" mother asked, trying to hide her surprise.

Raymond answered glibly but sincerely, "He said, 'O Lord, we thank Thee for our food and Raymond.' "

☐ A Sunday school teacher dramatically portrayed the Day of Judgment. "Fire will flash across the heavens. Thunder will roar. An earthquake will open the ground to open up gigantic floods which will sweep people away."

Piped up a little girl, "Please—will we get off from school?"

☐ A veteran Sunday school teacher, a lady who was known as a strict disciplinarian, entered the hospital for surgery. A few days after the operation she received this card from her class of juniors. "We wish you a speedy recovery. Vote five to four."

TAXES

☐ An American and a Hollander were comparing their flags. They found them quite similar. Said the Dutchman, "You have stripes, and so do we. You have red, white and blue, and so do we. And like you, when it gets near tax time, we feel blue. When our bill comes we turn white. When we pay it, we see red. Only in your country you see stars, too!"

☐ A little boy wrote a letter to God asking for one hundred dollars. The post office sent the letter to the White House. The president had a secretary send five dollars to the boy. The boy then wrote a thank-you note. "Thank you for sending me the hundred dollars I asked for. But why did you have to send it through Washington? Those birds down there deducted 95 percent of it."

☐ An Internal Revenue Service agent phoned a pastor: "A member in your church, Mr. X, has listed a donation of three hundred dollars on his income tax form. Do you know if he made that contribution?"

Came the pastor's reply, "I don't have the church records before me. But if he didn't, he will!"

☐ Q.: Did you know that when Hoover was president he gave all his salary back to the government?

A.: The idea certainly caught on. Now they have us all doing it.

☐ The owner of a lovely home in the suburbs was cutting his lawn. A stranger sauntered up. "Beautiful home you have. Worth about twenty thousand dollars, I would think."

The owner straightened up. "More than that. It's worth every bit of thirty thousand. By the way, are you looking for a new home to buy?"

"No," replied the stranger, writing down some figures in his little black book, "I'm the new tax assessor."

TELEVISION

☐ A tourist in a lonely backwoods country asked one of the old-timers if he thought it would rain.

"Will pour much," the old-timer predicted. The rain came down in torrents. The next trip into the area, the tourist spotted the same old-timer, who remarked, "I can't tell about the weather today. My TV's broke."

☐ First lad: Our TV is broken. The man is coming to fix it.

Second lad: How will he do it?

First lad: Oh, he'll probably open it up and pull out all the dead cowboys.

TEMPTATION

☐ A boy was told by his father not to go swimming. The father caught him swimming. "I didn't mean to go swimming," pleaded the boy.

"Why did you bring your bathing suit?"

"Oh," replied the boy, "I brought it along just in case I was tempted."

☐ Two new employees in a large warehouse were assigned work on the second floor. At the end of the first work day they headed for the door which they thought led to the stairway. But it was the door to the freight elevator. Mike opened the door and stepped into space, for the elevator at that moment was in use. A moment later he thudded to the bottom, surprised and bruised.

Pat, about to follow, hesitated at the sudden disappearance of Mike. "How are the stairs?" he called down.

"Not too bad," moaned Mike, "but watch that first step. It's a big one!"

☐ A man was telling how he overcame temptation. "I was in the village store and had a chance to steal a big bag of flour while the storekeeper was out of sight for a minute. But I resisted the impulse," he said virtuously, "and just took a loaf of bread instead."

TEN COMMANDMENTS

☐ The headwaiter in the cocktail lounge in the headquarters hotel for the denomination's annual convention remarked, "These people came with ten-dollar bills and the Ten Commandments—and they haven't broken any of them."

☐ An old chieftain was being evangelized by a missionary. Noting that the men had the habit of filing their teeth to sharp points, the missionary put emphasis on the "thou shalt not's." Patiently the aged chieftain listened.
"You mean that I must not take my neighbor's wife."
"That's correct," said the missionary.
"Or his oxen, or his elephants."
"That's right."
"Or I must not dance the war dance and then ambush him on the road and kill him."
"So right."
"Then I can become a good Christian," sighed the chieftain; "for I cannot do any of these things. I am too old."

☐ When a Sunday school class was asked to write out the Ten Commandments, one boy put down for the fifth, "Humor thy father and thy mother."

☐ An enthusiastic church member said to her pastor, "I'm so anxious to make a trip to the Holy Land, climb to the top of Mount Sinai, and shout out the Ten Commandments!"
The pastor replied, "I've got a better suggestion: stay home and keep them."

TESTIMONY

☐ In a testimony meeting a sour old Christian, noted for his lack of growth in grace, rose to tell of his experience. "Forty years ago," he began, "the Lord filled my cup with the water of life. Since then, not a drop has run in and not a drop has run out."

Just then a little boy on the front row said in a stage whisper, "My, I bet there's a heap of wiggle-tails in it!"

☐ Week by week a deacon in his testimony would exclaim, "O for the wings of a dove that I might fly away and be at rest."

One night, unable to stand any longer the repetition, a worshiper was heard to mutter, "Stick another feather in him, Lord; and let him fly."

☐ A clerk looked up to see a suspicious-looking man push a note in his direction which read, "Put all your cash into this bag, and don't say a word or I'll shoot."

The teller meekly slid back the bag filled with money plus a note of his own which read, "Straighten your tie, sloppy; your picture is being taken."

THANKFULNESS

☐ A miner who worked deep in the coal mines of Wales and who was known for his profanity became a Christian. His fellow workers, wishing to test the reaction of a new convert, stole his dinner pail. Expecting an angry retort with plenty of swearing, they were surprised when he smilingly replied, "Praise the Lord! I've still got my appetite. They can't take that!"

☐ A man rose from his seat in a crowded bus so a lady standing nearby could sit down. She was so surprised she fainted.

When she revived and sat down, she said, "Thanks."

Then he fainted.

☐ A man didn't know what to buy his wife for her birthday. Setting out to shop for something "different," he found the solution to his problem in a pet shop. Here was a very rare, and very expensive, talking bird—the Mexican wordy-bird. He ordered it crated up and sent to his home with the note, "Happy birthday, darling."

A few hours later he called his wife to find out whether his present had arrived and how she liked it.

"Just fine," came the reply. "It's in the oven right now."

Well, the husband was appalled and astounded. "But that was a very rare talking Mexican wordy-bird," he exploded.

"Oh, it was?" she said sweetly. "He didn't say one word to me."

☐ A petite farmer's wife was struggling hard to get her donkey to pull its heavily loaded wagon up the hill. Noticing her predicament, the village preacher got behind the cart and pushed it over the top.

"Thanks so much," she gratefully said. "I'd never have made it with just one donkey."

TIME

☐ Husband (waiting for wife to leave for church): For the umpteenth time—are you ready to go yet?
Wife (yelling): Why don't you keep quiet? For the last hour I've been telling you I'd be ready in a minute!

☐ A man brought before the judge said his occupation was calendar making. The judge said, "Then you'll understand my sentence: thirty days hath September, April, YOU, and November."

☐ A newcomer to heaven asked an angel how long a minute was up there. Came the answer, "A million years."

Then the newcomer asked, "How much is a nickel worth in heaven?" The angel's answer, "A million dollars."

Then he asked, "Would you please lend me a nickel?"

And the angel's answer, "Gladly—in a minute."

TITHING

☐ Years ago a man promised God a tithe of his income as the Lord prospered him. The man's first week's pay was ten dollars, of which he tithed one dollar. Promoted, he later earned one hundred dollars a week; then two hundred; and then three hundred. One day he asked to see his pastor. He told him how many years ago he promised God he would tithe; then he asked, "How can I get released from that promise? You see, it's like this: when I made that promise I had to give only a dollar a week, but now my tithe amounts to thirty dollars a week, and I just can't afford to give away money like that."

The old pastor looked at his friend, then replied, "I'm afraid I cannot get you released from your promise. But there is something we can do. We can kneel right down and ask God to shrink your income to the point where you will again have to give only a dollar a week."

TONGUE

☐ An elderly lady, well-to-do but quite deaf, purchased the latest model hearing aid. A month later she returned to the store to report that she could hear what people said, even in the next room.

When someone suggested how happy her relatives must be with her improved hearing, she chuckled, "Oh, I haven't told them yet. I've been doing quite a bit of listening, and I've changed my will three times!"

☐ An old philosopher of Greece once received a severe tongue lashing from his wife. When he listened in silence, she was the more infuriated; so she picked up a pail of cold water and threw it over him, drenching him from head to foot.

With the water still dripping from him, very calmly he remarked, "After that thunder and lightning I rather expected a shower."

☐ Lawyer to man whose car had been struck by a lady driver: I'd settle if I were you. After all, it's your word against hundreds of hers.

156

☐ A soldier at an army camp received a small phonograph record from his girl friend. Not owning a record player, he searched till he found one on a shelf in a tiny room at the service club. He closed the door, turned the record on, and found out it was a love message. He sat back enthralled at the terms of endearment, "Honey, I sure miss you."

Suddenly a soldier appeared at the door, looked in a moment, then went away. When the record was almost finished—and several fond expressions later—the same soldier reappeared. "I wonder," he hesitated, "if you realize your record is going out over the public address system to the whole camp."

☐ A golfer was trying to get out of a trap. Another golfer kept talking away, finally commenting, "The traps on this course are very annoying, aren't they?"

"Yes," said the first golfer; "would you mind closing yours?"

☐ A young man wishing to win the good graces of his rich uncle sat down in front of his uncle's parrot. "My uncle's a great guy," said the young man. "In fact, he's the greatest guy in the world." After adding a few more compliments, he paused, then laughed, "There, that ought to convince the old geezer!"

Later in the day, as the uncle sat in his easy chair, the parrot started in "My uncle's a great guy; in fact he's the greatest guy in the world." The uncle's face beamed with delight. As more compliments were repeated by the parrot, the uncle may even have thought of changing his will in favor of his pleasant nephew. Then there was a pause. Then came forth the parrot, "There, that ought to convince the old geezer!"

☐ A man who caroused on Saturday nights began to attend church every Sunday morning. Naturally, the pastor was pleased. "How wonderful it is to see you at services with your wife every week!"

"It's this way," said the husband, "I had to make up my mind—and I decided I'd rather hear your sermon than hers!"

☐ Finnegan, a railroad engineer of few words, phoned his report of a train derailment as follows, "Finnegan to Flannegan: off again, on again, Finnegan!"

☐ "What's more clever than speaking several languages?"
"Keeping your mouth shut in one."

TRAVEL

☐ 1st person: I'm afraid to travel by train.
2nd person: Why?
1st: Didn't you hear about the terrible train accident last night?
2nd: No, what happened?
1st: A plane fell on it!

☐ One lady said she was afraid to travel by plane. She explained, "I like terra firma. And the more firma, the less terra!"

☐ As the passengers tightened their safety belts before take-off, over the intercom came this announcement. "This is a recording. This plane will fly by automatic control. We will take off by automatic control, select our route, and land by automatic control. Everything possible has been done to insure your safety. Nothing can go wrong—go wrong—go wrong—go wrong—!"

☐ A stunt pilot offered to take up a Scotchman and his wife free on one condition—that neither of them would say a word. If either uttered a sound, they would have to pay twenty dollars at the end of the ride.

The Scotchman agreed. For two hours the pilot dived and circled and did the loop-the-loop, but not a sound came from the other seat. When they landed the pilot congratulated the Scotchman for his silence. "Thank you, sir; but I sure almost talked when my wife fell out an hour ago!"

☐ 1st person: Isn't it funny—when we send something by car we call it a shipment?

2nd person: And isn't it strange—when we send something by ship we call it a cargo?

☐ A little girl in New York City on a holiday was taken onto the elevator in the Empire State Building. As they sped past the seventieth floor, she blurted out, "Daddy, do the angels know we're coming?"

☐ One hundred preachers had chartered a plane for their convention in Los Angeles. As the plane flew over the Rockies the "Fasten-your-seat-belt-sign" flashed on.

As the stewardess passed by, one preacher said, "Tell the pilot all will be well, for there are one hundred preachers aboard."

"He knows that," replied the stewardess. "He said he would rather have four good engines."

TREASURERS

☐ At a sideshow in a little town a strong man squeezed a lemon dry and offered a reward of five dollars to anyone who could squeeze another drop out of the lemon. A little fellow came forward, took the lemon, and began to squeeze. To the amazement of all, a drop fell, then another, and a third. The astonished strong man asked, "Who are you?"

"Oh," replied the little fellow, "I'm the treasurer of the local church!"

☐ The treasurer of the Ladies' Aid took some money to the bank. She said to the teller, "Here's the aid money."

Hard of hearing, the teller thought she said, "Here's the egg money," and replied, "It's surprising what a bunch of old hens can do, isn't it?"

☐ Out in the Canadian prairies a preacher received his pay in the form of offerings placed in a box at the back of the church. On blizzard Sundays he received nothing. For three full weeks he was snowbound. On the third Monday, with his food supplies almost gone because of no money, he saw someone shoving through the snow. When he saw it was the church treasurer, his courage increased. He thought, "The church hasn't forgotten me!"

The starving minister opened the door and warmly welcomed his guest. Then the treasurer stated his business. "I just came to find out the address of the Old Fashioned Revival Hour. I've been blessed by their broadcasts the last three Sundays, and I just wanted to send them a few dollars for their radio work."

TRUSTEES

☐ 1st person: I read that soon scientists will make it possible to heat an apartment with one lump of coal.

2nd person: Our trustees have been heating our church that way for years.

☐ Because the church lighting was dim, the pastor asked the chairman of his Board of Trustees for a new chandelier. Months went by but nothing happened. When the pastor asked why, the chairman said there were three reasons.

Number one—they could not record this matter because no one could spell *chandelier*. In the second place—nobody knew how to play one. And in the third place—what the church really needed was a new light fixture!

☐ In the middle of a Sunday morning service a pastor announced that his Board of Trustees should remain after the service. A lady who came in after the announcement heard him comment at the close of the service, "Remember—the board should stay." When she remained after the benediction, the pastor explained that this was a meeting of the board. Replied she, "That's why I stayed; I'm bored!"

☐ A seminary student on his first Sunday in his first church, wishing to make a good impression, arrived early to get the hymn books out and the pews dusted. Noticing a dog in the aisle, he kicked the animal out. It made a yelp as it scampered out the door.

After the sermon a deacon said, "You may as well pack up."

"Why?" asked the new pastor.

"You kicked the dog out."

"What's so bad about that?"

"That dog belongs to the senior trustee."

Hurrying over to the senior trustee's home, the new pastor apologized.

The trustee admitted that he had been mad at first, but said, "Now I'm not mad. I wouldn't have wanted my dog to hear that sermon for a hundred dollars."

☐ Trustee (of large church situated on busy downtown corner, on trip to Africa and getting his first glimpse of the Sahara Desert): My, what a place for a church parking lot!

☐ At a business meeting the church was discussing the need of a new building. Though most were agreed on the necessity of a new structure, the decision needed the approval of a wealthy trustee, who got up to announce, "It's true that the old church is in need of extensive repairs, but I think we can get by without erecting a new building. To repair the old one I'll subscribe a thousand dollars." A heavy man, as he sat down he jolted the building. A big hunk of loose plaster landed on his head. Momentarily stunned but soon regaining his senses, he leaped to his feet and exclaimed, "This building is in far worse condition than I ever dreamed. I'll make it two thousand."

As he sat down, another member was heard to mutter under his breath, "O Lord, hit him again."

TRUTH-TELLING

☐ A prison chaplain asked an inmate, "What was the cause of your downfall?"

The inmate replied, "I was ruined by untold wealth."

"What do you mean by that?" asked the chaplain.

"Wealth I should have told about on my income tax report."

☐ The manager of a department store overheard a clerk say to a customer, "No, we haven't had any for a long time."

Rushing to the scene, the manager assured the customer, "We'll get it for you right away. We'll send out and get some."

Then turning quietly to the clerk, he ordered, "Don't ever tell a customer we are out of anything. Tell them we will get some right away."

"But," protested the clerk, "we were talking about rain."

USHERS

☐ An usher, nervous because this was his first time on the job, noting that the usual seat of an influential churchwoman had been taken, blurted out, "Mardon me, Padam. Your pie is occu-pewed. May I sew you another sheet?"

☐ The head usher was instructing a youthful volunteer in the fine points of his job. "And remember, young man, we have nothing but good, kind Christians in this church—until . . ."

"Until when?" asked the new usher.

"Until you try to put someone else in their pew."

☐ In church for the first time, four-year-old Johnny was given last-minute orders by his eight-year-old brother. "They don't want you to talk in church."

"Who don't want you?"

"The hushers. They're the ones."

☐ A minister in the pulpit saw a man in a back pew with his hat on. He motioned to an usher, who went to the man and asked him if he knew his hat was on.

"Thank goodness," said the man, "I thought that would do it. I've attended this church for six months, and you are the first person who has spoken to me."

VISITATION

☐ A preacher was visiting a man in an oxygen tent in a hospital room. He asked the patient how he was. The patient merely grunted. The pastor asked some more questions. On each answer the patient seemed weaker. Finally the pastor asked if he had any message, giving him a pad and pencil under the oxygen tent. The man wrote something, then died.

Realizing the importance of a man's last words, the preacher looked under the tent and read these words, "You are standing on my oxygen line."

☐ A group of Sunday school teachers were given instructions on how to do visitation. Two or three of them showed obvious timidity about the assignment. The pastor suggested they spend a few moments outside a home praying about the call.

When the group returned later to report on their calls, one of the teachers thanked the pastor for his suggestion to pray. He said, "Before each call I prayed the people wouldn't be home, and they weren't."

☐ A church had printed a form on which persons could ask to see a minister. Several categories were listed for possible checking so that the minister would know why he should call. The members distributed these forms around town.

A few days later the minister received through the mail a logical reply from a prisoner at the local jail. The category checked was "shut-in."

☐ A minister was calling on parishioners late one afternoon, about the time the men came home from work. Knocking on a door, he heard a woman's voice call out, "Is that you, angel?"

Came the pastor's immediate reply, "No, but I'm from the same department."

☐ "I'm going to be busy upstairs," mother said to her little girl. "Call me when the butcher delivers the meat."

A few minutes later the minister came calling. The lassie called up, "Mother, a man's here."

The mother called down, "Give him five dollars out of my purse, and tell him I didn't like his beef last week."

☐ Woodrow Wilson's father was a minister. Rather tall and thin, Wilson, Sr. made quite a contrast to his horse, which was well built. One day with horse and buggy and young Woodrow along, the minister was asked by a parishioner, "Reverend, how is it that you're so thin and gaunt while your horse is so fat and sleek?"

Before he could reply, young Woodrow exclaimed, "Probably because my father feeds the horse and the congregation feeds my father!"

☐ The minister had just comfortably settled in an easy chair when little Susie came running into the living room. Wishing to make a good impression on her visitor, the mother asked the child, "Please get that book your mama just loves to read."

A minute later little Susie came back in, lugging the big Sears catalog.

☐ The minister's little girl was put to bed early with a mild cold. When she asked to see her father, mother replied, "Daddy's busy in his study tonight."

When she asked a second time and got another refusal, the little girl said in solemn tone, "I'm a sick lady and I must see my pastor at once."

☐ One morning the parsonage phone rang. A minute later the hatless, coatless preacher ran out the door. His wife wondered what could be the matter. She thought of all the sick and offered a silent prayer. She was consumed with curiosity till she was able to ask him on his return, "Whatever was the matter?"

Naming a parishioner who lived down the street, he replied, "She phoned me because the end of the world was coming. She saw 'Peace' in the sky. But when I looked up I saw "Pepsi" written by a skywriting plane."

☐ A pastor and wife took their two-year-old daughter on a call. In the living room of one of the parishioners, the little girl ran her finger across the floor, and holding it up, yelled, "Dirty, dirty!"

☐ Two road workers, Protestant and Catholic, were making repairs when a priest passed by and entered a saloon. "Isn't that a shame?" observed the Protestant workman. "A man of the cloth has no business in a saloon. He should be visiting the sick."

Just then a minister entered the same saloon. The Protestant workman remarked, "There must be somebody pretty sick in there."

☐ A minister was asked to visit a sick lady who was a well-known worker in another denomination. When he arrived he mentioned to her ten-year-old son, "I'm wondering why your mother called me when she is an active member in another church. Is your minister away?"

"Oh, no," replied the little lad. "Mother is afraid she might have an illness that's catching."

WEDDINGS

☐ A seven-year-old was asked, when attending a wedding, what kind of wedding he was going to have. Solemnly he answered, "I'm never going to marry. I've lived with married people too long."

□ A young jeweler was being married. The minister asked for the ring, then gave it to the jeweler to put on his bride's finger. "With this ring . . . ," prompted the minister.

"With this ring," the bridegroom nervously repeated, then added, "we give a written guarantee, promising the customer that the price will be refunded if it is not satisfactory."

□ "How did the wedding go?" the preacher's wife asked.

"Fine," replied the preacher, "till I asked if the bride would obey and she said, 'Do you think I'm crazy?' and the bridegroom in a sort of daze mumbled, 'I do.' Then the fur began to fly!"

□ Little Lori at a fashionable wedding didn't miss a single detail. She saw the bride come up the aisle with her father, then go down the aisle with the groom. "Mother, did the lady change her mind? She went up the aisle with one man and came back with a different one!"

□ An usher was passing the collection plate at a big church wedding. A well-dressed lady looked up, most puzzled. Without waiting for her question, the usher nodded his head, "Yes, madam, it is unusual; but the father of the bride requested it."

WIVES

□ A Canadian newspaper carried this letter in one of its columns: "I read with deep concern that the Church of England is going to omit the word 'obey' from the new marriage service. May I ask if this new church rule will be retroactive? [Signed] Nervous husband."

□ Pat asked Mike what they meant by *phrenology*. Mike said, "They feel the bumps on your head and tell what kind of a man you are."

Pat replied, "If they examined the bumps on my head, they'd know what kind of a wife I have."

☐ Said one wife, "My husband's the meanest man in the world. He'd been stone deaf for three months before he told me."

☐ A small boy, meeting his grandmother for the first time, asked her, "What makes you a grandmother?"

She replied, "My dear, you have two grandmothers—one on your mother's side and one on your father's side. I am your grandmother on your father's side."

The little boy looked at her silently a moment, then said, "Grandmother, you won't be here a week before you'll find out you're on the wrong side."

☐ Wife: I thought you were going to the lodge meeting tonight.

Husband: I intended to, but it's been canceled. The wife of the Grand Invincible Exalted Supreme Potentate won't let him out.

☐ "My wife had to be beautiful but dumb," said a man deeply in love. "Beautiful that I should fall in love with her. Dumb that she should fall in love with me."

☐ Husband: My wife and I get along well together. Even when we are out in the automobile we cooperate beautifully. You see—I steer while she drives.

☐ Policeman: Did you see the number of the car that knocked you down, madam?

Woman: No, but the woman in it wore a black hat trimmed in red, and her coat was imitation fur.

☐ On a mountain trail in the Andes a traveler met a farmer riding on a mule, while his wife trudged along behind him. "Why isn't your wife riding?" the traveler asked.

"Because," the farmer answered, "she has no mule."

☐ 1st wife: How would you describe Father's Day?
2nd wife: Just like Mother's Day—only you don't spend so much.

☐ Young husband: This pie is burnt. Send it back to the store.
Young wife: I didn't buy it. It's my own cremation.

☐ Church bulletin: "A new loudspeaker has been installed in the church auditorium. It was given by one of the deacons in honor of his wife."

☐ A man was asked, "Does your wife pick your suits?"
He answered, "No, just my pockets."

☐ Wife: I know all my husband's stories backwards.
Husband: And she tells them that way, too.

☐ A women's liberation rally was in progress. One speaker bellowed out, "The time will come when women will get men's wages."
Her husband in the crowd was heard to mutter, "So true. Next payday."

☐ A lady stood beside a car on a busy highway, looking helplessly at a flat tire. A passing motorist stopped to help, muttering, "This is no job for a woman."
When he had changed the tire, the woman whispered, "Please let the jack down easy. My husband's taking a nap in the back seat."

☐ A wife who was always nagging her husband passed away. She had given instructions as to what to put on her gravestone. It was "Rest in Peace." The husband told the tombstone salesman to chisel in those words and then add, "Till We Meet Again."

WORK

☐ Lady (to new maid): Somehow you don't seem to be getting things clean in the living room. Do you use the vacuum?

Maid: No, ma'am. It spoils the television programs for me.

☐ A tramp knocked on a door and asked for something to eat. The owner told him he would give him a meal in exchange for some work. "See that pile of wood in the back? I would like you to saw it."

The tramp replied, "You saw me see it, but you don't see me saw it."

☐ A well-to-do man remarked, "I believe in hard work. I have two hundred thousand dollars. I have it because of hard work and the hundred and ninety-eight thousand my uncle left me."

WORRY

☐ When Philip D. Armour, packinghouse magnate, was a young man establishing himself in business, he became heavily involved in debt.

One day his banker called on him. "I'm worried about your loan at our bank," he remarked.

"Well," the young man replied, "no use both of us worrying about the same thing."

☐ A Methodist bishop was sitting at his desk worrying about the state of church affairs in his parish. It was nighttime. He was troubled, wondering which course to take, until the big clock struck midnight.

He said that he seemed to hear the voice of the Lord, "Now go to bed, bishop. I will sit up the rest of the night."

☐ A radio commentator covering an important news event was at the point of cracking from strain. A colleague, observing him tensely gripping the microphone, suggested he take a tranquilizing pill.

"I can't," he replied. "If I'm not tense, I get nervous."

YOUTH WORKER

☐ A new youthful preacher arrived at a church to take up his pastoral duties. The number of young ladies in the youth group increased considerably, probably because he was unmarried.

When someone suggested he might marry one of these young people, he answered, "Oh, no; for then I would break up my Christian endeavor."

☐ The new youth worker, a stickler for keeping himself in top physical shape, found himself so busy he neglected to do his daily exercises now and again. So one day, on an errand in downtown New York City, he ran behind a bus for nearly a mile. Arriving back at the church all out of breath, he explained to the church treasurer who happened to be in the office, "I ran behind a bus and saved fifty cents."

Replied the treasurer, "Why didn't you run behind a taxi and save three fifty!"

ZEAL

☐ An elderly lady, poor in this world's goods, was rich in enthusiasm for the Christian faith. Though she belonged to a staid, dignified church, she often burst out with a loud "Hallelujah," much to the dismay of the church officials.

So the elders took counsel and approached her with this proposition. "If you will not disturb the peace of our church service by shouting 'Hallelujah,' we'll give you two large, warm blankets."

Desperately needing the extra cover, she agreed. But next Sunday morning she heard some glorious Bible truth and couldn't contain herself. Out came a loud "Hallelujah!" Two elders sitting near her gave her a stern look.

For a few minutes she was quiet. Then another wonderful truth gripped her heart and she just caught herself in the nick of time from emitting another word of praise. But five minutes later, when the preacher spoke words that again thrilled her soul, she broke forth with, "Blankets or no blankets, praise the Lord, Hallelujah!"

☐ Superintendent: Why are you carrying only one piece of wood when the other men are each carrying two?

Worker: Perhaps they're too lazy to make a second trip.

☐ When young and just converted, D. L. Moody used to fill up a pew in a rather aristocratic Boston church with street urchins. Many of the upper-crust church members resented this intrusion. When Moody tried to join the church, the board discouraged him. "Think it over for a month," they advised. "And pray about it, too."

They thought that would be the last they would see Moody. But they failed to take into account his indomitable drive, for next month he appeared before the board again. Rather taken back, they asked, "Did you do what we suggested? Did you pray about it?"

"I did," Moody quietly replied.

"And did the Lord give you any encouragement?"

"Yes," said Moody, "He told me not to feel bad because He has been trying to get into this same church for the last twenty-five years, too."